WORTHY

Learning to Date in a World
That Tells You You're Not Enough

CLARISSA CHRISTENSEN, MS, LPC

ISBN: 978-1-7341294-0-3

Edited by: Katie Chambers of Beacon Point LLC

Cover Design by: Jeannine Rivera of JovialcoloR

Hey, Friend!

I'm so happy you're here!

You have chosen to take the first steps in creating a single life full of passion and purpose. That's a huge deal, so congratulations! You are well on your way to leading the life you will love.

This book is just the beginning. Head on over to my website, www.igniteyourworth.com, and check out the other resources available to you.

I'd love to connect with you! You can contact me via

Email: igniteyourworth@gmail.com

Instagram: Clarissa_christensen

Do you want some **FREE** bonus handouts to help you on your journey to self-worth? Of course, you do! Check out my Facebook group, Ignite Your Worth with Clarissa Christensen, to get exclusive materials.

To my parents, Kenny and Anita, for always
supporting my crazy ideas. I love you both!

To my sweet friend tribe. You guys are the best!

To anyone in my life who's ever loved me, as well as those who
have hurt me. This story wouldn't be possible without all of you.

Contents

Acknowledgments

It is by the grace of God that I was able to write this book and go through this journey. I am so thankful for a God who is constantly pursuing me, loving me, and calling me to do big, scary things.

Thank you to everyone who has supported me during my writing adventure. You all are a blessing to my life. A special thanks to my parents, my Friday night girls who constantly make me laugh when I feel like crying, my accountability partner/soul sister, Jocelyn Jones, and my cousin Melissa for being my daily wake-up-keep-me-sane phone call. I love you all!

To Jeannine Rivera of Jovial Color for my beautiful cover design. She worked tirelessly to capture the exact look I was going for. I can't thank you enough!

Also, a huge thank you to Chandler Bolt and the whole Self-Publishing School Community for guiding my process and offering so much support.

Introduction

"How to date in a world that tells you you're not enough."

That just feels like a big title, and if I'm being honest, it really scared the crap out of me when I wrote it down. Dating in this swipe right, swipe left culture can be really challenging and defeating. You can get super excited about a guy and next thing you know, you've been ghosted. Or maybe you're like me and you've dabbled in online dating only to find out that it's super freakin' exhausting.

But what if you don't even know where to start with dating? What if you're the person who's sitting at home on a Friday night while your friends are out with their boyfriends, fiancés, or husbands and you're feeling left behind. Maybe you don't even feel like you deserve a healthy, positive, and loving relationship.

"Now, Clarissa, why would anyone not think they deserve good things?! That just sounds ridiculous!"

It's a more common thought than most people would like to admit. Most of us have made questionable choices at some point in our lives and now we have this mental story we keep

telling ourselves over and over. The story might sound something like, "I'm not good enough," or we might feel emotionally tarnished in some way, which leaves us feeling
undeserving of the type of relationship we've always wanted.
So now we only date people with low standards like our own,
and we date well below what we want and need for ourselves.
Is any of this sounding familiar?

Before we jump right into the meat and potatoes of why being
single isn't so bad, allow me to introduce myself. My name is
Clarissa Christensen. I am a woman of God and a licensed
professional counselor (in private practice for five years). I'm
also a Catholic, a daughter, a friend, and an extroverted introvert. I love all things sparkly and rose gold. Chai tea soy lattes
are my jam and contemporary Christian music is my obsession
on any given day. Fashion, changing my hairstyle, and playing
around in makeup are creative outlets and hobbies of mine. I
also love singing and performing (unless I'm being put on the
spot). Something else you should know about me? I happen to
be single.

I guess you could say I've been single my whole life with the
exception of a few relationships sprinkled in here and there.
For the last seven years, though, I've been on my own. I used
to look at being single as the equivalent to having the plague.
It was an unwanted disease, and you were lucky to make it out
alive! OK, maybe that's a little dramatic but you get what I'm
saying. It wasn't until a few years ago that I realized being
single is a huge blessing. Before you think I'm crazy, just hear
me out.

My life has gone through so many ups and downs over the last
ten years. I earned two college degrees, worked my butt off for
my state counseling license, bought a house, turned around
three years later and sold that house, moved into a studio
apartment, learned how to live small, lost some very important

people in my life, started a business, traveled to new places, went on a handful of really bad dates (and a couple good ones), and the list goes on. I can't imagine what it would have been like to go through all of that while trying to maintain a healthy romantic relationship.

Relationships are work. Yes, they can be wonderful and beautiful, but they are also a lot of work. I mean, think about it. A healthy relationship includes a fair amount of selfless love. While a partner can add love and support to your life, they can also distract you from your goals and be one more thing to maintain. Before you start protesting, I'm not anti-relationships. I am very pro positive, healthy relationships. Now I don't know about you, but it's a challenge to give of yourself to your coworkers, clients/customers, friends, family, classmates, homework, etc. during the day. And when you get home, sometimes you just want to focus on you. You are done giving.

I've been there for the last seven years. Emotionally exhausted from my class work, internships, and work commitments. I feel very fortunate to have been able to unapologetically focus on myself and my goals without feeling like I'm sacrificing time with a spouse or children.

It took a lot of prayer to surrender my single life over to God. For six out of the last seven years, I tried to be in total control of my love life all the time. I thought that if I was in total control, I would have more peace about my life. Ummm, big fat no.

While I was accomplishing my business and personal goals like the boss babe that I am, I felt incredibly anxious about dating—like thinking about it all the time and never knowing what dating site to be on or how long to talk to a guy before expecting or accepting a date. If I felt creeped out by online dating, did that mean this particular guy I was talking to was giving me bad vibes or was that just normal? **So overwhelmed**.. If you ask any of my good friends, they will tell you what a nut case I was. Can you relate?

About a year ago, I made the choice to turn over my single life to God. It was a heavy load I was tired of carrying alone, and I knew I would continue on a downward spiral if I didn't give it all over to Him. If I could trust God with every other aspect of my life—and see the fruits of that effort—why not let Him make my single life and dating life fruitful?

Letting go was going to be an adventure, and I was ready for it! Throughout this book, I'm going to take you on my personal journey to figuring out how to live a single life full of purpose, wonder, and beauty. I hope you're ready; it's going to be a fun ride!

I found this quote that has been such a sweet reminder of God's love and goodness. The author is unknown, but it reads, "Obedience is rooted in **trust** that the One guiding me is guiding me into something GOOD." Amen and Hallelujah! Insert some praise hands 'cause I'm all about it!

Moving forward, I want you to look at me as though I am your best friend, your big sister, an older, wiser, been-there-done-that-picked-up-the-pieces-telling-you-what-not-to-do-so-you-can-be-successful-in-your-dating-life type of person.

Some of what we talk about in the chapters to come might sting when you read it. It might even trigger thoughts about a negative past experience you might have had. Get ready to feel some big emotions.

It's my hope and prayer that you will walk away from this book feeling encouraged and empowered to make choices that reflect the deepest desires of your heart. I want your eyes to be opened to knowing your worth so you can stand firm in your beliefs and not take crap from people who are just trying to use you. I am going to be suuuuuuuper vulnerable with you as I tell parts of my own story, and I hope you're comfortable with that.

I want you to know that you're not alone in this. If you're like me, and most of your friends are in relationships, it can feel very isolating being left on the outside. But have no fear, my friend, we're going to walk this journey together, and it's going to be awesome!

My goal is that this book will help you redefine yourself, live authentically, and be a boss at setting boundaries around your relationships. I want you to learn how to discern which relationships are good for your life and set dating standards that you can actually stick to.

By the time we get through this journey we're taking together, I hope you'll be thriving in your life. I want each and every one of you to be living a life of passion and purpose—a life that you love, with a tribe of supportive friends who want to hold you accountable to dating and marrying the man of your dreams. Sounds great, right? Let's do it!

Please note, the names and details used throughout this book have been changed to protect the confidentiality of the individuals involved.

Growing into Insecurity

I n order for you to understand how I got to where I am today, you need to know where I came from. I'm currently a strong, confident, loving, and passionate person, but I haven't always been that way.

Even though I'm six feet tall, I used to try to make myself invisible. Think Princess Mia in *Princess Diaries* pre-makeover. I didn't think I was pretty, and I had zero style, no confidence, and no idea who I was. I only had a few friends and, overall, just felt really lost and alone for most of my middle-school and high-school years.

I grew up in a home with my parents and my older sister. My dad works in the farming industry, and my mom quit her job as a first-grade teacher to be a stay-at-home mom. We lived in what I would call a middle-class home in South Texas, surrounded by pastures with grazing cattle on three sides and farmland on the other.

When my sister was going into second grade and I was starting pre-K, my parents made the choice to homeschool both of us. My dad's busy season at work was during the summer, so while my sister was in public school, it was challenging for us to have quality family time unless she was pulled out of school. I'm smiling right now thinking about how unbelievably blessed we were to have a full-time mom who loved the heck out of us. I learned so much from her, and I am the woman I am today because of her and the huge sacrifice my parents made for her to stay at home with us.

Being homeschooled was cool because my mom's sister also chose to homeschool her four kids. We were all close enough in age to get together for collaborative assignments and field trips. It was really fun because it felt like I had a lot more siblings since we were together so often. Art projects, PE class, playing in the dirt, climbing trees (them not me; I'm a scaredy-cat), and eating corn dogs were all part of our school time together.

Most people who hear about that part of my upbringing have the impression that I've lived a charmed life. Don't get me wrong, 95 percent of my life has been great. I'm definitely not complaining. But while much good came from being home-schooled and having my family close to me all the time, there were also negative aspects that went along with it. I could be both blessed by my supportive family but also feel extremely lonely and out of place.

After going through grad school to become a therapist, working with clients, and finally going to see my own therapist, I realized some of the main reasons I so desperately needed a guy's attention to validate me. The big "AHA!" moment of my life if you will: I was bullied.

I was bullied my whole childhood life. What? How, Clarissa? You were homeschooled? You were supposed to be sheltered from all the bad things of the world. I know, I know. I must be extra special to be able to have been bullied within my controlled environment. Let me give you the rundown.

I can remember my mom encouraging me and then sometimes volun-telling me (you know, when someone *tells you* that you're volunteering for something) I was going to attend church retreats when I was in middle school. When I got to high school, I became a teen leader of those retreats. It feels weird to say it, but even though I was involved in these events for many years, I didn't feel like I fit in. Everyone was nice to me, but I was constantly trying to make new friends and connect. Yet, I didn't feel like I could get all the way into the cliques that already existed. My feelings were frequently hurt because my efforts to nurture relationships weren't returned. I found myself exhausted after these events because I was putting so much energy into making small talk or trying to look and act cool . . . whatever that meant. This is just one example of the loneliness and rejection I felt.

Oh, did I mention I was also the overweight kid? Most of my clothes came from Walmart or a plus-size store. My outfits typically looked a little too mature for my age, so I wasn't the most fashion-forward kid and teenager. If they made a big and tall store for kids and teens, that's probably where I would have shopped. I was always insecure about what I wore and how people saw me because everything I had was so different from my sister, who inherited the skinny genes along with the rest of my cousins. I definitely got called names and made fun of for my weight. I had no idea how deeply those hurtful words would end up wounding me. The teasing started my feelings of worthlessness and rejection. Since I was one of the only chubby kids in most activities, I always wondered if my weight was the reason I wasn't accepted. I was nice and kind, like everyone else. My weight was the only difference I could see between myself and them.

I grew up in a world without Pinterest fashion boards and style influencers on Instagram. Nobody was telling me how to put on makeup or dress for my body shape. I felt lost. My mom was great, but she's about six inches shorter than me and her "fat jeans" are a smaller size than I've ever worn.

On top of it all, I should add that I was not coordinated, so I couldn't even earn cool points from playing sports. Even trying to play kickball with my cousins was a nightmare because I was so slow. I got picked last and everybody knew we were probably going to lose if I was on their team. So, I didn't play. Looking back, I was really isolated. I didn't have the emotional maturity or feelings vocabulary to put my feelings into words, but it's true all the same. I had a hard time connecting with the people I was around. It felt like I was going to drown in a sea of insecurities, and nobody would even notice I went under.

It's super cliché to say this, but I'm going to say it anyway: I was the black sheep of my family. I'm not as outdoorsy as my extended family. I'm the artsy one in the family. I love being creative in any capacity, whether it's through singing, art projects, or cooking. So, it was really hard to relate to my friends and cousins since our interests were all so different.

I mentioned having an older sister earlier. Well she and I are also extremely different. She was the thin, popular one who always had a boyfriend, and I wasn't any of those things. Aside from having the same parents, I really think that's where our similarities stop. That sounds dramatic, I know, but we really are very different. She's the super outdoorsy, get dirty doing yard work type of person, and I love everything indoors —unless I'm sitting by a pool!

My sister and I didn't have the best relationship growing up. She didn't treat me well. She loved her independence and I was the annoying little sister she was forced to cart around everywhere. When we went out together, she would never introduce me to her friends, or even act like she knew me. I'm sure I was the absolute most embarrassing person in the world to her, and I can only imagine all the cool points she lost having me in tow.

You always hear people talking about blood being thicker than water and siblings being each other's best friends, but that wasn't the case for us. I didn't feel accepted or wanted by her. I didn't feel good enough. As a kid, that totally and completely crushed me. I tried to figure out what I needed to change about myself to make her like me more or want me in her life in a deeper, more personal way, but I could never figure out what I was doing wrong. Eventually, I just stopped trying and accepted our differences. It took me a long time to realize that we don't have to be best friends in order for me to love her and have her as my family. It's absolutely OK that we don't love all the same things and want to spend time together 24/7. Just because our personalities don't blend well, doesn't mean either of us is a bad person. Sometimes it just ends up that way.

By this point in the story, I'm sure you can tell I wasn't popular at all and I craved connection all the time. I felt like I was constantly looking for a place I might be able to fit in and belong. No group of friends ever felt quite right and I found myself clinging to the two or three friends I managed to make.

I never dated in high school. Well maybe there was that one date with that one guy who ended up liking my other friend and dating her. Then there was the whole collection of guys I had crushes on who ended up dating my friends or someone else. It was rejection piling on top of rejection.

Fast forward to college and my desperation was in full swing. I related to that Johnny Lee song, "Looking for Love." I really *was* looking for love in all the wrong places and looking for love in too many faces. After experiencing so many years of rejection, I was thrilled to have some attention from guys. It didn't matter who they were or if it was positive or negative attention. Attention is attention—or at least that's what I thought.

The sad part is that once I got some attention, I knew I liked it but also didn't fully believe the compliments I received. You think I'm pretty? *Why?* You want to take me out? *What for?* You like spending time with me? *That's a first.* I had all these lies in my head that I wasn't worthy of anyone's time or energy. To this day, I have no idea if the interest from those guys was genuine or not.

During my first two years of college, I accepted dates from several guys who didn't have my best interest at heart. In the process of trying to find my community in this new place, I began dating a guy from one of my classes just a few weeks into my first semester. Things began to progress in our relationship. He was not a Catholic like me, or even Christian, and had very negative friends who talked nonstop about their drug use and sexual encounters. After a couple of months, my roommate told me she had witnessed him cheating on me while I was out of town. He was apparently a go big or go home type of person because he didn't just cheat once, he cheated on me three times with three different girls, all in the same weekend. Needless to say, I quickly broke up with him. All my friends told me I deserved better. I agreed with them, but on the inside, I questioned what I did wrong. If I was enough, wouldn't he have stayed with me? What was wrong with me that he felt the need to go out and create dating experiences with someone else? More rejection, bigger insecurities.

I was ecstatic when a guy from Bible study showed interest in me. He's in my Bible study, so he's got to be a good guy, right? He convinced me that we should have a secret relationship so our friends wouldn't judge us because he was younger than me. My young and naïve self agreed to his request. To make a long story short, my roommate had to break the news to me that "Bible study boy" was dating me but had also been in a long-term relationship with another girl, which was the real reason our relationship had to stay a secret. I was unknowingly the "other woman," and the amount of guilt I felt about my role in his life made me feel sick to my stomach.

Learning I was the other woman, from one of my best friends at the time, was heartbreaking and oh-so-embarrassing. I wanted to crawl under a rock and hide for about ten years. Honestly, when I found out, the thought of crawling under a rock and never coming out sounded great. Thinking back to that season of my life, I'm reminded of Proverbs 27:6, which says, "Wounds from a sincere friend are better than many kisses from an enemy." The hurt from my best friend's words only lasted a short time, while the impact of the situation haunted me for several years. I'm very fortunate to have had friends in my corner who were looking out for me and showing me I was worth so much more than the shallow interest from that guy.

Since at the time I couldn't recognize my worth, I was a magnet for toxic relationships. I really felt like I had hit a low point in life and didn't understand my value or what my purpose in life was.

My poor connection with my sister, the shallow relationships with various boys, and the struggle I had to connect deeply with friends in high school all shared a common theme. They all reinforced the worst belief system that I had about myself: I wasn't good enough, I wasn't worthy of someone's time, I wasn't valuable as a human being, I wasn't special enough to be someone's first choice. I could justify why every guy didn't want to date me and why my sister didn't want to be my best friend. I continued to put up walls to protect myself from getting hurt again. I didn't want to open up and show people the real me and truly put myself out there. I didn't think I could handle one more person rejecting me. The rejection I experienced cut deep. Deeper than I could have ever recognized at the time, and I had enough.

2

Lions and Tigers and Online Dating, Oh My!

My Story

Those first two years of college were pretty rough in the dating department. I would get all dressed up for a date only to have the guy pick me up looking frumpy and take me to his smelly dorm room to watch a movie. Could he not see I brought my outfit A-Game? Knowing I didn't want to go down that same road again when it came to meeting guys, I thought I'd give online dating a shot. Several people in my life had used various dating websites with great success, so I didn't think I had anything to lose by trying it.

I not only joined the dating site a few of my friends were on but asked around and joined several other free sites, too, just for the heck of it. Getting on multiple online dating sites while having the lowest self-esteem ever is a great idea! Said no one.

Oh Lord, y'all. I was the hot mess express of online dating. I was looking for validation from anyone who would give it to me. I used the multitude of messages from guys as a way to tell myself that I was worthy of someone's time and love, so it was soul crushing to find out these guys messaging me were just looking for a quick hookup and nothing meaningful.

That wasn't the type of attention I was looking for. I wanted someone who looked at me in a way that said, "I want to fully know and love you selflessly." Not "You're an object to be used." I wanted attention from someone who wanted to protect my heart from pain, not someone who caused it.

Can we just take a moment to acknowledge that online dating just might be the actual worst thing ever invented? I know it has its upside, but have you spent any time thinking about the process of online dating? It's like buying shoes online. The picture may be pretty, everything on the outside meets your desires, but when they come in the mail, they just aren't a good fit. The same applies to online dating; it's so challenging getting to know a person's heart when all you can see are their stats.

My heart was aching for genuine love, and I was fooling myself into believing those shallow emails from guys would come close to filling the void. I would devote myself to email exchanges with guys, and just when we would talk about meeting, they'd ghost me. Poof. They disappeared into thin air. Every time it happened, I was so incredibly disappointed. It was another way I felt rejected and not good enough. Consumed with obsessive thoughts about myself and what I could change to make these guys more interested in me, I constantly questioned my body and whether guys would want me because I wasn't as thin as other girls. I was always updating my profile with new pictures or new information to see if that could reel in more guys. My self-esteem continued to plummet to a low level I didn't even know existed.

I had been using the dating sites for several months when I was about to give up hope of ever meeting a quality person. Did I mention that, at the time, my level of patience ranged anywhere from zero to negative twelve? Just when my site subscription was about to expire, I hit a plot twist!

About five months into my online dating adventure, I ended up meeting a really fantastic guy. Mr. Right and I were in a long-distance relationship, which I can say would be a challenge for any couple, but it felt especially hard in the fragile early stage we were currently in.

When he and I met, I was staying with my parents over summer break, and due to them living in the middle of nowhere, Texas, I didn't have any Wi-Fi. You're probably thinking this was twenty years ago. Nope, just seven. My parents didn't feel the need to upgrade from dial-up. For those of you reading who were barely born during the days of dial-up, it was basically just one technology advancement up from the stone ages. So, Mr. Right and I spent our first week communicating through the dating website's email option and would send multiple novel-sized emails a day back and forth to each other, all while burning through my cell phone data plan. It was so fun to feel all the giddiness and butterflies that always seem to come with the start of a new relationship.

After a week of emails flying back and forth as quickly as we could send them, Mr. Right finally asked for my phone number. I thought I was going to pass out! I was so nervous to take the next step toward a relationship. Just in that first week, I could tell he was very different from the other guys I had previously dated.

We texted and called for the first month of getting to know each other. Our calls would last for four or five hours every night, and I couldn't believe I had found someone so incredible. I had never connected with anyone as well as I connected with him.

After a month of talking on the phone, I was back in Denton

and, praise God, now had Wi-Fi. So, we planned our first Skype date. That may sound super cheesy—and let me tell you, it most definitely was. Side note, the great thing about Skype dates is only the visible parts of you need to be presentable. I definitely had a cute top on and wore makeup, but I also wore pajama pants and only straightened the front part of my hair. I'm sure I looked hilarious if you had seen me in real life!

The date went great, so we started planning a trip for him to come to Texas so we could finally meet face-to-face and not screen-to-screen. Oh great, I would have to actually put real pants on for this one! A sacrifice I was willing to make.

He was a trooper for this first in-person meeting. I wasn't comfortable having him stay with me or meeting him alone (we did meet on the internet after all). So, he agreed to fly to Houston and let my parents pick him up—yes, my mom and dad met him before me—and then we stayed the weekend at my parent's house.

All I can say is the weekend was magical. We went out to dinner, danced outside under the stars with no music, and he spent time getting to know many of the important people in my life by being my date to a friend's wedding. The weekend ended with a very tearful goodbye as I dropped him off at the airport on my way back to Denton. I'm not even joking. I basically had to run out of the airport and ended up crying for the first two hours of my drive. When the tears finally stopped, I called my mom because, of course, I wanted to know what she thought of him.

She and my dad really liked him, which I couldn't have been happier about. She asked if I thought he was "the one." I told her I did, and to my surprise, she didn't question it. She could also see Mr. Right was someone special.

Everything looked great between us on paper. We relied heavily on technology as a way to stay connected. Over the course of the year that we dated, we only spent about three weeks' worth of time together in person. I was in my senior year of college, and he was working a job with an inflexible schedule. We were madly in love and somehow the distance felt romantic. Kind of like Romeo and Juliet without the death scene.

Or so we thought.

We had long talks about getting married and starting a family one day. I remember telling my friends it was just easy with Mr. Right despite not living in the same state.

The funny thing about long-distance relationships is they don't allow you to see each other in your day-to-day, natural habitat. He and I would bring our best selves to our visits, and while the visits were great, we spent more time sightseeing and going on dates than figuring out the logistics of our future together. We were able to overlook some major red flags, like the fact that neither of us wanted to move out of our home states. Umm hello, did we think we were going to have a long-distance relationship forever? Come on, Clarissa. Nonetheless, we pressed on with a "love conquers all" attitude, naively thinking everything would work itself out.

The moving issue was just one example of the red flags I encountered and ignored. Now, I want you to understand that when I say red flags I don't mean dangerous situations. Through conversations with him, he would say things that made my stomach drop because they were issues we didn't agree on. Instead of speaking up about these things in the moment, I would put them aside and tell myself, "I'm sure he just misspoke. I'm sure he doesn't actually feel that way. Wait, did he just say that? I probably heard him wrong." I made up every excuse I could think of in an effort to keep this relationship going.

At this point, you might be questioning why I didn't just let him go. That's a great question. You see, we had already talked about a future together. We had talked about getting married, the type of house we wanted, how many kids we wanted. We had picked out those kids' names and had gone ring shopping. We fell in love hard and fast, and I felt like I was in too deep to know how to get out.

When we were on the phone with each other, he would frequently ask me to marry him and I would say yes, every time, knowing that it wasn't the actual proposal, but we kept making that promise to each other over and over again. We were engaged without the ring because we were too broke to afford one. I didn't want to tell anyone about our conversations of marriage, which was yet another red flag. I told myself I wanted it to be a special secret between the two of us. We were secretly engaged, and it was something just the two of us had. When in reality, I didn't want to tell anyone because I think I knew deep down that it wasn't going to work. I knew I couldn't marry someone who had some significantly different beliefs from me, but I wanted so badly to stay with him long enough for him to become the person I wanted him to be, instead of seeing him for who he was. I kept hoping he would change for me.

My need for validation led me to ignore the fact that he was not changing and had no intention of changing. I kept telling myself to give it time and he would come around. I can be pretty persuasive, so I thought after a few conversations I could begin molding his beliefs, but he never became the person I wanted him to be.

I'm sad to say, the relationship ended just a year after it

started. I hope you never have to experience a breakup over video chat.

It was so hard to get closure afterwards. Crying and not being able to comfort one another was wrenching. There was no last hug goodbye. It was two hours of pure hell, talking about every deal breaker of our relationship and seeing if either one of us would be willing to compromise our desires and beliefs. Two hours of saying, "But I love you; this can't be over."

That night, the relationship wasn't the only thing I lost. The breakup took all my confidence and happiness with it. I felt like a shell of a person. I thought I was going to marry this man and start a family, but now what? This is the Romeo and Juliet death scene I mentioned before. Even though there wasn't a physical death, I was having to grieve the loss of a year's worth of hopes and dreams. I was absolutely devastated. I felt worthless. I looked in the mirror and hated the girl looking back at me. She was an emotional wreck. She was lost.

One of the main reasons I pushed off the breakup for months was out of fear. If it took me twenty-one years to find him, how long would I have to wait for my next boyfriend? Would I find anyone else? Should I settle even though I know I wouldn't be as happy as I could possibly be with someone else? Maybe I was being too picky and my standards were too high. What if I'm alone forever? I can't be alone forever. There aren't any stories with endings like, "and then she lived happily ever after all by herself." Disney never made that movie! These were all the thoughts that kept circling my brain leading up to the breakup and some of these thoughts even continued after the fact.

For six months after the breakup, I had so many regrets about that relationship. I blamed myself for why it ended and thought God was punishing me for not making good choices, for not discerning more. Turns out, God is a loving and gracious God and he doesn't work like that. He can make all things work for His good.

I can now look back and say that the breakup was one of the best things my ex and I could have ever done for each other. He and I were not ready for a serious commitment like marriage and kids. I truly believe he and I were not good for each other. We weren't communicating well and struggled to talk about hard topics, like relocating, all while I was attempting to sneakily change his core values. Sometimes you can have two people who are fantastic individuals but together make an unhealthy couple. My insecurities fueled an unhealthy environment.

I don't want to give you a bad impression of my ex. He was an incredibly wonderful, thoughtful, and loving person. Our relationship and everything that went wrong should not reflect badly on him. It wasn't fair for me to think I could change him when nothing was wrong with him. Had I been more emotionally stable at the time, I would have been able to let him go, but my own insecurities convinced me I needed to change him and had me thinking he was the problem. I never took the time to look in the mirror and ask myself what part I was playing in my pain.

God was trying to tell me during the whole relationship that my ex wasn't the person he had for me, but I was too stubborn to listen. If I'm being honest, I really knew about four or five months into the relationship that it wasn't going to work. Sometimes the things we want just aren't good for us, and we have to be honest with ourselves about that.

After the breakup, the thought of being alone was too scary, and I thought being in a mediocre relationship would be better than not being in a relationship at all. Friends, that is so false. An unhealthy relationship only causes more stress, more insecurity, and more suffering. It does not build you up and bring you joy in the ways a healthy one can.

Once again, I went searching for validation via online dating. How long did I wait before getting back online, you ask? A week. Surely that's enough time to get over a year-long relationship. I could only move forward! Please tell me you're laughing at how ridiculous this all sounds. I was insane to think I would have fun on a date just one short week after a major break up. I had always heard you have to date someone else to get over the last guy you dated, so I thought I would give it a try. Boy oh boy, was that a terrible idea.

I think I hold the title for Queen of Bad First Dates. Seriously, give me a tiara because I've earned it! That first date after the breakup would have been bad no matter what since my emotions were all over the place and my heart was still filled with deep, raw pain.

My date took me to one of those all-in-one kind of places where you could bowl, play putt-putt golf, laser tag, arcade games, and eat. This guy (let's call him Bob) had such an ego. I'm not competitive at all, but I talk smack because it's fun. I told Bob I would crush him at putt-putt. Bob played golf in real life, so obviously I knew he would be better than me due to all of his bragging about his skills (insert eye roll). Long story short, I crushed him like a Ritz cracker. He got mad because he was taking it all so seriously, and I was just trying to have fun.

Our conversations sucked because we had nothing in common. We made awkward small talk as we played a couple of rounds of putt-putt, and yes, I won both times. I was ready to call it a night when he suggested we go to dinner. I was so stunned that he was having a good time, I forgot how to decline an invitation and ended up being stuck for another hour in the blind date from hell.

We ended our date with dinner at a steakhouse, where I found out he only suggested the place because he had a gift card he wanted to use up (face palm). Through almost complete silence, I ate my meal as quickly as I could. We awkwardly hugged goodnight and I drove myself home, crying the whole way.

That date only reinforced how much I loved my ex and wanted to get back together. Once again, I found myself stuck in this place of worthlessness, feeling empty. I didn't know who I was or what I wanted. I just wanted the pain to go away. I wanted to feel normal again.

I believe it was about six or eight months after the breakup when I saw my ex was dating someone else. His best friend and I had remained in communication off and on, and I still had the false hope that my ex and I would get back together after I finished grad school.

When I saw he had a new girlfriend, I suddenly felt like it was a competition to see who could move on the fastest. (Super healthy thought, Clarissa.) I feel like a lot of us have been there, thinking we need to move on first and date someone who is cuter than the person we broke up with. Geez. No. Just no.

Reflection

Are you feeling stuck in the competitive breakup mindset? If you are, be mindful that it often turns all of our desires for a future spouse into superficial, prideful desires. If you're sitting in this mindset , I encourage you to hit pause on your life. Ask yourself:

- Why do I feel this way?
- Are you seeking to validate your worth by how quickly you can move on?
- Are you trying to somehow punish your ex by no longer being available?

These thoughts lead to toxic actions. Your challenge is to sit in the feelings of the breakup. If you aren't currently going through a breakup, I want you to reflect on how well you think you handled your last one.

- Did you find closure?
- Do you feel like you're still carrying around baggage that you need healing from?

- Could you wish that person well and want good things for their life even if it doesn't include you?

Take the next few pages to write down your thoughts. Remember, be as honest with yourself as you can.

Journal Page

Take Action

I fear some of you reading this chapter may have realized you are in a relationship that isn't going to work out. You want to break up but aren't sure how.

Having a support system is key during this time. If you have family and friends who support you and your need to end your relationship, lean into them. Give yourself permission to borrow their emotional strength when you feel like you don't have any.

If you don't have a support system but still feel the need to talk about your relationship, now is a great time to find a therapist. If you are connected to a church, you could also seek some pastoral counseling. Whatever you do, don't go at it alone. It will be much easier to back down if you don't have accountability.

3

Swipe Right When You're Lonely

My Story

S wipe right when you're lonely.

Have you ever done it? I can't tell you how much time I've wasted over the years just mindlessly scrolling dating apps with the swipe right or left feature. If I think too hard about that time in my life, I get really down about it. I spent so much time looking for guys when I could have been nurturing my current friendships. By the time I started dating in college, I had developed a fairly large group of supportive friends. We'll talk more about them later, but the point I'm trying to make is that I had so many people I could call upon if I was feeling lonely. I wasn't using my resources; instead, I was turning to apps to try to fill a void and validate my existence.

I have a lot of friends who have met their spouses through online dating sites and apps, so I'm not trying to say they're evil or anything like that. Everything is not for everyone. It's OK if your best friend meets all of her boyfriends online, but it doesn't seem to work for you. I want to dig into the reasons why I believe it's not a good fit for certain types of people. I want you to be able to give yourself permission to stop online dating if the process doesn't feel productive for you.

My online dating journey began by signing up for one profile on one site. After my ex and I broke up, I went off the deep end. I had a hard time sitting alone with myself because I was so used to being in constant communication with my ex all day, every day. Being in my silent apartment was really hard for me. The negative thoughts I was having about myself just got worse and worse the more isolated I was. In an effort to help silence the negative thoughts, I joined any and every online dating site I could find. I was constantly communicating with someone new.

I literally had no standard for who I would talk to. It didn't matter what I wanted out of a boyfriend, or whether the latest guy possessed any qualities I liked, I would talk to them. I don't think I had intentions of going on dates with most of them. I just liked the validation in the moment. Most of the guys were very complimentary of the pictures I had uploaded and the flattery was nice; however, not all messages had nice intentions.

I was frequently sent inappropriate nude pictures or crude messages with detailed descriptions of how the guy would want to use my body. It was disgusting.

I signed up for all the dating sites so I could be open to any of the possibilities out there, but in turn, just opened myself up to more people who were tearing down my self-esteem one message at a time. I came to think the only purpose I could serve was to use my body to give pleasure to a guy and that nobody would want anything else from me. I didn't feel like I had anything else to offer. I praise God daily for protecting me against the evil that was present in that time in my life. I always blocked the guys who sent the inappropriate pictures and messages. But even so, those experiences were emotionally damaging and really stuck with me.

I went on dates with guys I knew I would have no future with believing the lie, "Casual dating is fine. Nothing bad can come of it. They don't need to have any dating potential because it's just a date."

Causal dating can be a great way to get to know what your preferences are for a future spouse. However, before you start casual dating, get to know yourself and your needs. Know your heart. At my core, I'm not a casual dater. I never have been. I've tried it enough to know that about myself. I'm a relationship person. I love everything about relationships and casual dating just gives me constant anxiety. Every. Single. Time. I never know if the date will become more than just a date and I usually get attached to people quickly. Dating without intention is a nightmare for my mental health.

Something else that came from casual dating is the fact that it ignited my desires for a relationship. It would remind me of how much fun dating someone is, and my heart ached to date someone I actually cared about, who also cared about me in the same way.

My online casual dating adventures also fueled my hatred toward my single life. All I wanted was a relationship but kept coming up dry. Nothing would stick.

Can we just talk about ghosting for a minute? If you're unfamiliar with the term, it's when you're in the early stages of dating or getting to know someone and they just dissolve into thin air with no warning. It's a super weird thing that's just been made so much more possible with online dating.

What purpose does ghosting serve, you ask? If you're the one doing the ghosting, it avoids the uncomfortable "I'm just not interested in you anymore" type of conversation. Ghosting is a passive and cowardly action. If you've done it to someone, you know it doesn't feel right. If you've been ghosted before by someone you know, it leaves you questioning everything. Maybe you've been ghosted after having sex with someone. That's extra painful. You feel used and misled for so many reasons. You feel like not only your time was wasted, but your body was used—and it was all for nothing.

Having people ghost me perpetuated my feelings of worthlessness, which made me run back to the dating sites to get validated by other men, to then get emotionally torn down again and be left with even less self-worth. It was a vicious cycle.

Another reason I ran to online dating was because 97 percent of my friends were dating, engaged, or married when I was in my very early twenties. I had so many friends who were blessed to meet their sweet husbands at a young age. Looking at my life in comparison to their lives had me feeling like I was doing everything all wrong.

I finally figured out I needed to give myself permission to be single. It's hard. When I felt like I hit the very bottom of my rock bottom, which was actually about six feet under rock bottom, I went on a dating fast for a year. What's that, Clarissa? So glad you asked!

A dating fast meant I was shutting down all my dating profiles and accounts, not initiating any romantic interaction with guys nor accepting any romantic interaction and interest from guys. I would not go on any dates. The only guys I would hang out with one-on-one during that time were friends I had already established firm friendship boundaries with, and the ones who knew about my dating fast and respected it.

It was a wild experience, to say the least. I don't think I've had a year that tested me emotionally like that year. Like I mentioned earlier, I was wasting a lot of time on the social media style of "dating." In that year, I became a better friend within my existing friendships and made new connections. I was able to focus more on school, got my homework done without procrastinating as much, and took the time to get to know myself.

That year of fasting was completely transformative in my relationship and walk with God. I had so much extra time now that I wasn't swiping right and left for hours. I could actually pray regularly. I was in a Bible study with some great girls, went to church more often throughout the week, and allowed my heart to be open to hear what God wanted for me.

I've never been good at trusting God with my single life, and I'm still not great at it. I always say that was the year I dated Jesus and allowed Him to date me. The void I mentioned earlier was the piece of my heart reserved for God. The reason I felt empty was because that void can't be filled with anything that doesn't belong there. Filling it was other guys versus time with the Lord was why I felt so unfulfilled.

That year of getting to know the Lord and myself better was the beginning of finding myself. It was the start of really defining my dating goals, standards, and boundaries. I decided that, if I wanted more out of my dating life, I was going to have to set a high standard for myself and not self-sabotage those standards. I needed to learn how to be assertive and not apologize for having and respecting my own boundaries.

OOF!

I've been working on boundary setting for five years and even still, as I type this, I feel anxiety creeping in. If you're the peacekeeper, like I tend to be, you understand how hard it is to put yourself first. People pleasers very rarely put themselves and their needs first because they worry, "What if they get mad at me? What if they don't like me? What if they go away and don't want to be my friend or boyfriend anymore?"

Those are all scary thoughts. Let me tell you right now, healthy relationships don't grow out of a place of scarcity. Resentment, regret, and general dislike of people grows in that insecure place. The great thing about expressing and setting boundaries is that it lets your true friends show up for you in the ways you need them to. It also lets you know who your true friends are. Friends who are healthy and supportive want to respect you and your boundaries. I had to let that sink in for a while before I was able to let go of a few of my friendships that weren't good for me.

Now that I was able to identify that, I needed help. I had to establish a support system that would help me be accountable in my weak moments, a group of friends who wouldn't try to take advantage of my natural desire to do anything for anybody at all cost. I needed therapy, and I needed it now.

I was a broke college student and ended up working through a lot of my issues while becoming a counselor in grad school. I did eventually get myself to counseling a few years later which was so helpful. I regret not prioritizing money in a way that allowed me to get to counseling sooner.

Up to this point, we've talked quite a bit about how I got to the low points in my life. You've walked with me through being bullied, through a devastating breakup, through the rockiest of the rock bottoms of online dating, and to me finally realizing I had some big issues with my self-worth. Maybe you're finding yourself in a very similar place in life right now and have been saying, "me too" along with my story. So how about we switch gears and talk about how I pulled myself up from the impossibly low pit?

Get ready to jump into your own vulnerability right along with me! Getting to a happy place in your single life can be really challenging. You have to feel an overwhelming amount of negative emotions that most of us don't enjoy experiencing. Let's take a minute to pray together. These next few chapters can be transformative for you, but before you read them, I want you to make a commitment to yourself and to God that you will be open to hearing His will for your life.

Prayer for Openness and Healing

God, I come before you feeling alone and broken. I don't want to feel this way anymore. I want to feel your overwhelming love for me today and every day. Please help me to see the actions I'm doing that are hurting me. Help me to see the toxic relationships in my life. Guide me to your will for my life. Help me to remember your intense love for me. I want to know a life that is full of your love, grace, and forgiveness. Help me to learn how to give myself grace in my life while I'm on this healing journey. Amen.

Reflection

Take the next couple of pages to write down any toxic people and/or situations that came to mind while you were praying. Give yourself some time and space to identify these people and situations before moving on to the next section of the book.

Journal Page

Take Action

Is online dating for you? Answer the following questions to help you determine if you have healthy boundaries around online dating, or if you need to give yourself a break.

1. Do you obsessively check your phone and/or dating apps? Yes_____ No_____
2. Do you talk to anyone and everyone who sends you a message? Yes_____ No_____
3. Are you feeling pressure to go on as many dates as possible? Yes_____ No_____
4. Do you feel suffocated trying to manage all of your messages? Yes_____ No_____
5. Do you feel negatively about yourself because you don't have a lot of messages in your inbox? Yes_____ No_____
6. Do you feel isolated or depressed while online dating? Yes_____ No_____
7. Would meeting someone in person feel more authentic to you? Yes_____ No_____
8. Does the idea of taking an online dating break give you peace? Yes_____ No_____

9. On a scale of 1–10, how high is your
   anxiety / nervousness with online dating? Circle one.
   1 2 3 4 5 6 7 8 9 10

If you answered yes to five or more of the first eight questions, I would encourage you to take a week off from online dating. Delete the apps so you aren't tempted to look at them—you can reinstall them again later if you need to. After your week away, rate your level of anxiety again and see how it differs from last week. If the level is significantly lower (three or more levels), online dating may not be the best place for you in this phase of your life.

If you are feeling overwhelmed by your online dating experiences, I want to encourage you to seek professional counseling to help you get to a healthy mindset before returning to the dating apps / sites. If you aren't sure where to start, you can email me at igniteyourworth@gmail.com.

4

Redefining Myself

My Story

I figured the first step to redefining myself would be to turn to God. I wanted to know who he said I was. So, I went to the Bible and found several passages that really spoke to me. I want to share a couple that I love the most.

Genesis 1:27 says, "So God created mankind in his image, in the image of God. He created them; male and female he created them."

I'm in awe of that verse every single time I read it. I can't get over the fact that we all look like God in some way. He created us to look like Him. Thus, all the lies I believed about myself when I was younger just can't be true. I can't be ugly if I look like God. He created me with a specific design in mind.

John 3:16–17, "For God so loved the world, that he gave his only Son, that whoever believes in him should not perish but have eternal life. For God did not send his Son into the world to condemn the world, but in order that the world might be saved through him."

God loves me enough to send his son to die for me?! That verse never gets old.

I have a shirt that says, "God is madly in love with you," and I believe that with my whole heart. God never leaves us. He's always faithful and steadfast in his love for us. While I was in the middle of my dating fast, I remembered something I'd heard before: God never imposes; he always proposes. We have the free will to choose his love and delight in it, or we can reject it. He never forces himself on us, and that makes his love all the more beautiful in my eyes.

Based on scripture, as a child of God, I am made worthy, I am chosen, I am loved, and I am enough. God chases us down and has fought for our love. He sees our imperfections and places a great value on us in spite of them. We don't have to be perfect because he doesn't expect that. God said we were worthy of the ultimate sacrifice of his son's death.

Like woah.

If I'm all of those things as a daughter of God, then why the heck am I giving so much emotional power over to my haters, my users, and my abusers?

We must stop believing the lies that we aren't good enough as we are. However, just because you *are* enough as you are doesn't mean you need to stop growing as a person. What I mean is that as a daughter of a King (Jesus), you deserve to be treated like a princess and no person on earth has the right to mistreat you.

Some of you reading this may be feeling like you're not living for the glory of the God, either by how you lived in the past or how you're living now. You may feel ashamed of those parts of your life. Well, I'm here to tell you that we serve a loving and gracious Heavenly Father who is forgiving and just wants your heart.

One of my favorite things about being Catholic is our ability to confess our sins to a priest and get a fresh start. I know my friends in other denominations confess their sins to one another, so they are held accountable to those sins. If you aren't Christian, the power of having accountability is still open to you through good friendship. I don't want you to think you are excluded from a better way of life. You are loved.

Before we move on to setting your dating standard, I want you to say the following affirmations to yourself. Say them out loud, unless you're in an airport or something. I guess that could be a little weird.

- I am loved
- I am chosen
- I am enough
- I am the daughter of a King
- I deserve more than mediocrity
- I deserve to be adored
- I deserve to have a healthy relationship
- It's OK to want more for myself
- It's OK to not settle
- It's OK to live outside the social norms

During my dating fast, I was able to put a lot of thought into who I am with my identity rooted in Christ. I started thinking about what it would be like to date with this newfound identity. If my primary relationship is the one I have with God, that means I would be OK if a dating situation didn't work out. I found so much peace and comfort in this fresh relationship with God. Once I realized the stability I had with him, the pressure and anxiety to force a romantic relationship drastically decreased, though don't get me wrong: I was still looking for "the one."

Spoiler alert. There is no such thing as "the one." Did I just crush all your hopes and dreams about your love life? Good! Just kidding. I'm not heartless.

I'm constantly hearing people talking about how they cannot wait to find "the one." But then I got to thinking. What does finding "the one" even mean? Who is "the one," and how do I find him? What happens if I pick the wrong one instead of the right one? Did reading that give you just as much anxiety as it gave me?

Having the idea that only one person in the world could be a good spouse for you is a bit of a close-minded perspective. When I found myself thinking this way, I felt trapped. It seemed like an impossible task. The truth is, there are billions of people on the planet and in all actuality, any number of people could make a great spouse.

It seems really glamourous, romantic, and Lifetime movie-ish to fantasize about how you'll be out in the world one day and, from across a crowded grocery store, you'll see a guy and your eyes will meet as you both reach for the same bag of frozen peas, and then everything will magically fall into place. Of course, you hit it off because what else could bond your love together more than a mutual love of peas? Your love story starts. You get married. You have kids. And your life is amazing, and then you live happily ever after. Sounds perfect right? In case you haven't noticed, life is everything but perfect.

The thought of dating was still very scary to me, so I started to redefine my dating standards again. This go around, instead of writing down every quality I could ever want in a husband, I decided to separate the qualities between two lists: a non-negotiable list—the qualities that I would not and could not compromise on—and a list of preferences.

I think it's really important to mention that it's 100 percent acceptable to have a list of qualities that define your dating standard. I've been told I'm judgmental, I'm not giving guys a fair chance, I have the bar set too high and no guy would ever reach it . . . just to name a few.

But that just isn't true. I've dated enough to know the qualities I wouldn't be able to handle in a spouse. My big mistake with my last relationship was that I compromised my list and everything went downhill fast. I wasn't doing that again. And you don't have to either . . .

Maybe you've been desiring a higher standard for yourself but aren't feeling supported by your friends and family to make the change and break your cycle. Maybe, like me, you've heard some of those phrases before. You've been told you don't have the right to expect to be respected in the way you would like. Well, if you've been looking for a sign to move on and make some changes, this is it! Right here, right now, I'm giving you permission to set your bar high. You've just acknowledged you're the daughter of a King—that's got to change things, right? I hope so!

Now that you've given yourself permission to desire more out of your dating life and future spouse, let's talk about the two types of lists you're going to make. Your non-negotiable list is the must-haves of your relationship. Those things that are so important to you that resentment would build up inside of you and would ruin your relationship if you compromised on them. If you've never set a dating standard for yourself before, it can feel overwhelming, so I'll give you an example of a non-negotiable scenario.

Ginny is twenty-five and has dated a few guys before but

nothing's really worked out. She's a conservative, Christian woman who volunteers at her church every week and is an advocate for the pro-life movement. Having been raised by alcoholic parents who aren't in her life anymore, she doesn't drink or go to bars, but she's extremely extroverted and loves music.

Based on her life, here's an example of what her non-negotiable list could look like:

Christian

Pro-life

Politically conservative

Nondrinker

Extrovert who enjoys concerts

Trustworthy / loyal

Supportive of her volunteer work

Keeping this list in mind, it would be in her best dating interest to reject a date from Dave, a liberal atheist who smokes weed and likes to binge drink with his friends on the weekend. But what if he's supportive, loyal, and likes concerts? Doesn't that count for anything? Yes, of course. Dave is probably a wonderful person (just like my ex was), but if his lifestyle and core values are extremely different from hers, there isn't much dating potential there.

It's important to analyze your list and know if there's room to make a compromise here and there. Ginny could meet someone who checks off everything on that list but one. What if she meets Ben who's introverted, but because he really likes her, he chooses to go to concerts and becomes more social out of a desire to pursue her.

The key thing to remember is that sometimes people want to change and grow in healthy ways when they're in relationships. Ben could really love concerts with Ginny and enjoy that she brings out the adventurous side of him and embrace that instead of putting up a fight when she wants to go out. It's when we force people to change that problems can occur.

If Ginny is willing to compromise on the extroverted/introverted item on her list, that item needs to be moved to her negotiable list and not remain on her non-negotiable list. My rule of thumb is all the must-haves go on the non-negotiable list, and preferences go on the negotiable list.

Let's talk about the negotiable list for a minute. As I mentioned before, this list has qualities you prefer, qualities previous boyfriends had that you enjoyed but could also live without if the guy checks off well on your non-negotiable list.

Now that Ginny has established her non-negotiables, she's ready to work on her negotiable list. She's moved extroverted over and is ready to add some more qualities. Ginny likes to travel and hike, so she wants someone who will go on adventures with her. Men with brown hair and blue eyes are very attractive to her, so she adds that to the list. Ideally, she'd like a funny partner because she likes laughing with her significant other, and she enjoys cooking bold new recipes, so "adventurous with food" is her next item. I'm hoping you're seeing a trend. These are all things that would be less likely to make or break a relationship.

No guy is going to be perfect. Just like we aren't perfect. Perfection is never attainable. I beg you, please do not hold your dating prospects to the standard of needing to meet everything on both lists. That defeats the purpose of the lists altogether. You want to date the guy that has all the qualities that are most important to you and then be able to relax and compromise on the less important things. The examples I gave are just examples. Take them at face value. This is not me telling you what needs to be important in your life, I can't do that for you. Rather this is an encouragement to take some time to really think about your life and what's important to you at your core. I want you to sit down and consider what your deepest desires are for your spouse.

Are you a political activist that needs a partner in crime to join you at rallies? Are you a super chill introvert that enjoys staying home and making dinner instead of going out to bars? Are you highly educated and want someone who will challenge you intellectually? Are you an avid gym goer who wants a workout buddy? I say it again: think about what's important for you.

When you're thinking about your lists, think about the person's personality traits too. Do you want him to be funny, kind, caring, generous, authentic, trustworthy, honest, loyal, intelligent, a man of integrity, a provider, a protector, or wise?

You can absolutely add these types of traits to your list. When I say that to my clients so many of them say, "Well, duh, Clarissa. Of course I want him to be honest; that goes without saying." Ummm, does it? Not everyone believes they need to be honest with the person they're dating. Putting it on the list means it's on your radar. You'll be more likely to recognize dishonest people when you're looking for honest ones.

The same could be said for loyalty. Look at how he treats his friends and family. Has he had long-term friendships ever? Does he have healthy relationships with his family? Has he casually talked about being unfaithful in previous relationships? These are all different ways you can see his character and decide if he's someone you think you could stay committed to for the long-term.

If you say, "Yes, I want a man who can be a provider for our family." Great, how do you define provider? What does that word mean to you? Does that mean he needs to hold down a full-time job while you also work full-time? Do you have goals of being a stay-at-home mom? Is so, could his income and job aspirations afford that lifestyle for a family? These are great questions to ask yourself as you make this list.

More list-making tips!

When you're making your list and putting down qualities. Ask yourself:

- How do I define that word?
- What does that quality mean to me?
- Am I being too vague?

It's OK to be very clear and specific. In fact, I encourage it! In the next few pages, take some time to write down your non-negotiable and negotiable lists. Take as much time as you need before moving on to the next chapter. Feel free to come back to these pages at any time and make edits to your list as you think of more things to add or shift. The older you get, the more likely your needs are to change, and that's alright.

My list has gone through a few edits over the last seven years of being single. It's normal to make edits, especially when you're single and discerning. Please do not make serious edits while in a relationship. We don't shift our list to make the people we're dating fit. The people we're dating need to fit our lists.

Reflection

Have you ever avoided red flags or gut feelings in order to force a relationship? Yes_____ No_____

Have you ever compromised your core values while dating? Yes _____ No_____

If yes, in what way?

What are some qualities you would like to avoid in a future partner? You can list them below.

Take Action

Now it's time to make your list. Take your time, there's no need to rush through this process. Give yourself time to not only reflect on past relationships but also imagine your dream guy.

Non-negotiable list

Negotiable list

.

5

I'm Not Touching You

My Story

How many of you played that game with your siblings where you would almost be poking their eye out, but not quite. Taunting them with the almost-touch. As much fun as it was to be the one doing the taunting, it was so annoying when it's being done back to you, and your boundaries weren't being respected.

Now that you have redefined yourself in God emotionally, you need to define your physical boundaries. You've learned how to create and respect some pretty awesome emotional boundaries from making your negotiable and non-negotiable lists in the previous chapter, but how do you set physical boundaries?

It can be extremely challenging to stand up to your beliefs if they go against the current norms, like mine do. Saying no to certain things like sex is grounds for ridicule. You can be called uptight or a prude. Sex is driving our culture right now. It seriously feels out of hand. One-night stands, unprotected sex, middle schoolers getting pregnant. It's blowing my mind, y'all.

I talk about sex all the time with clients, and the more I talk to women and young girls, the more I realize so many of them don't want to dress provocatively or have sex with random people. They simply believe the lie that no guy will want them if they don't have sex on the first date. Or they have to "dress in a way that keeps the guy interested." I'm not going to lie to you. There *are* a lot of guys who will dump you if you don't have sex on the first date. If having sex under those circumstances violates your boundaries, then you need to let that man go. Better yet, you go. Walk away with a feeling of empowerment that you didn't allow someone to degrade you.

I feel like it's important to say you don't owe a man your body. No part of it. Someone once told me she had sex with a guy because he took her out to dinner at Olive Garden, and she felt like she owed him sex afterward because "he went above and beyond" by taking her out. That was so sad to hear. Is that really where the social standard is? Getting your dinner paid for is considered going above and beyond? Knowing someone for three hours means they have a right to your body?

What I love most about setting boundaries with people is the fact that it gives that person the chance to rise to the occasion or to get lost. Neither of you have wasted your time. Guys who see your worth can see you for more than what your body can do for them. They see you as a complete mind, body, and soul individual.

Growing up, I had the impression that sex was bad and the only reason you do it when you're married is to have kids. This skewed perception of sex is what has helped me keep my virginity. I'll just go ahead and out myself right now. I'm an almost-thirty-year-old virgin. So many people are extremely shocked when they find this out. Most people don't even believe me, which is honestly pretty insulting but understandable at the same time. I've had doctors push birth control and nurses think I was just saying I wasn't sexually active because my mom was in the office with me. Believe it or not, though, it's true and it's something I'm really proud of.

I can recall googling different things about my body or sex when I was in high school. Inevitably, I stumbled on porn sites and what I saw made me afraid to have sex. Everything I encountered was so abusive. One of my college professors was trying to prove a point about abuse in relationships and showed porn to our class. I just kept thinking, If that's sex, I want no part of it.

It wasn't until I was in college and participated in a Theology of the Body Bible study that I was able to fully grasp why I had this strong desire to hold my virginity so close and not give it up for just anyone.

If you aren't familiar with Theology of the Body (TOB), I'd encourage you to check it out. Everything about it is amazing. I could write a countless number of books on what I've learned from TOB, but for now I'll just paraphrase a portion that was hands down the most powerful thing I've ever heard about sex and my body:

It's not because our bodies are bad that we wait to have sex, it's because they are so good. God created us in such a profound way. Men and women's bodies fit together perfectly, and when they come together, they can create life.

Is there anything more beautiful than that? Our bodies just make sense together, if you really think about it. Sex outside of marriage can create so much unnecessary anxiety. As someone who has anxiety and has had my fair share of panic attacks, I don't want to add anything to my life that would cause more anxiety.

I truly believe our bodies are good, and beautiful. God created us, and I am embracing the reason he created our bodies. Like some of you, I fall into the category of Christians who have had to work through a lot of shame when it comes to sex and my body. TOB helped me realize that our sexual desires are not something to be ashamed of, but in the right context, should be celebrated and honored. I know a lot of you reading this are desiring to live a chaste life. I want you to feel encouraged and empowered in this mindset. It's not easy, but I'll share some of the guidelines and boundaries I've set for my own life and maybe they'll help you too.

Here come the big questions. "Clarissa, how do you not go all the way with a guy? How far is too far? Is it really bad to have sex before marriage? What about when you get engaged? It's OK then, right?" Such loaded questions! But ones I've personally needed to find the answer to.

How far is too far?

If you're asking yourself that question, then what you want to do is probably too far. Kiss, hold hands, be all cute with each other, but keep in mind, once you have sex, it's hard to not cross those boundaries again. You lose the sweetness of the cuddling because the new expectation is that things will lead to sex. Again, I repeat, know your boundaries.

What about when you're engaged?

If you recall, I was engaged before. If I had had sex with him, I know it would have been so much harder to end the relationship. I would have also had to live with the knowledge that I violated my own physical boundaries with him. Most of us learned in biology class that our bodies release hormones when we have sex. Sex is meant to create a deep intimate bond with one another. When we have sex outside of marriage and the relationship ends, it can truly feel as emotional as a divorce.

Is it really bad to have sex before marriage?

It's not my personal preference, but I won't shame you for engaging in premarital sex. There are some risks involved, and you need to be aware of them. Something so many people don't talk about is the big health risk you're taking by having sex with a multitude of partners. I personally don't ever want an STD; I'm not sure anyone does.

I want to do anything I can to reduce the possibility of contracting one. Abstinence is a great way to reduce your chances. Along with not having sex with random people, I make it a priority to talk to my dates about their sexual history. This isn't something that needs to be an uncomfortable conversation. If you can't openly talk about your sex life with a potential sexual partner, you aren't mature enough to have sex. Part of having healthy physical boundaries is knowing what steps are necessary to protect them. Communication plays a huge role in maintaining your sexual standards. We can't be afraid to talk about a topic that can impact our health and well-being on such a deep level.

I've heard that I make maintaining my purity seem easy. Well it's not easy, but I can give you some tips that have helped me make it more manageable. I'm going to use my personal boundary of not having sex before marriage for my examples.

The first tip, as I've mentioned, establish your boundaries. Once established, you need to let your potential romantic partner know your boundaries. For example, I told guys on the first date my personal boundary: sex is not an option while dating. If the guy isn't OK with that, I let him bounce before either of us gets too attached.

My second tip: don't set yourself up for failure. Lying in your bed with a guy, under the covers, with the door closed is just asking for trouble. It would be hard for anyone to resist that. Same goes for being home alone with your boyfriend. It doesn't matter if you're a teenager with raging hormones or an adult. Know yourself and your struggles. What is your internal motivation for remaining chaste? My motivation comes from a place of wanting to seek the Lord and all that pleases him. I know that holding myself up to a higher standard is better for me emotionally. It's in line with my core beliefs, and it's pleasing to God. Having that knowledge in my back pocket makes it easier to stop and not let intimate situations get out of hand.

Pro tip number three: Have dates out of the house. Allow the guy to pursue you and plan adventures. I see so many couples whose first date is a super late-night movie at home. I was talking to a previous client who had been dating a guy for almost a year, and she confessed she had never been on a real date. She never got to experience getting dressed up and waiting in anticipation for a man to come pick her up, or even the opportunity of being treated to a meal. Every "date" was a casual "hangout at home." I'm not saying the guy needs to pay for everything always—not everyone is in a stage of life to be able to afford that kind of dating lifestyle—but it's OK to want to see your guy putting in some effort to woo you.

The big kahuna of all tips is asking some friends to hold you accountable. My primary love language is physical touch, so it would be easy for me to let the physical aspect of a relationship get too far out of hand and leave me with regrets. I don't want the good elements of physical intimacy to overshadow the emotional and spiritual substance within the relationship. I love that my friends are the type to ask me how I'm doing in this area of my life. It's such a blessing because they aren't shaming me about it. They love me enough to help me stay strong in my personal desire to remain chaste.

The last tip, most people probably aren't going to like. And I can handle that because it needs to be said. Be mindful of what you're wearing. Let's think about lingerie for a second. The key elements of lingerie are that it's revealing, sexy, and a tease because it gives away most of what's underneath but not everything. Its purpose is to turn on your partner. If this is true about lingerie, then you want your daily wardrobe to be the opposite of that. The purpose of clothing is to cover your body. Your clothes don't need to tease or entice the opposite sex while you're dating. Before you get your panties in a twist, just hear me out. The female body is absolutely gorgeous. I think we can all agree on that. We truly have beautiful curves. You could be completely covered head to toe with fabric and your body would still be appealing to men. So, with that knowledge, let's encourage our fellow brothers in Christ to respect us and not help them lust after us. Let's dress in a way that encourages them to look at us with a loving respect because when they look at you, they see your face first, not your cleavage or your rear end hanging out the bottom of your shorts. And don't worry, I have no double standards here. I have the same beliefs for men. I appreciate their bodies so much. They are strong and built to protect. It's so easy to lust after a guy who has a nice body and is running around shirtless. I want guys to be mindful of that as well.

Reflection

- Take some time to think about what you want your physical boundaries to be.

- Have you been happy with the way guys have treated your body in the past?

- Have you ever felt violated by someone?

- Have you gone too far to the point of being uncomfortable or regretting your choices?

Take Action

It's OK to reclaim your body and start fresh right now with new boundaries. List your physical boundaries below and pick one to three friends who you fully trust to hold you accountable to them.

Accountability friends:

1.

2.

3.

6

To Be Seen

My Story

I have a feeling we're about to go through some rough waters with this topic of fashion and modesty. It can be quite controversial, and I'm aware I have very unpopular opinions compared to current social norms. This chapter is not meant to shame anyone but simply to get you to think about what you wear and how it might be affecting the people you love and/or your future spouse.

Before I go any further, it's important to say the following: it's never a girl's fault if she is sexual harassed or assaulted. So, let's just be clear on that.

I'm not in any way shaming a survivor of any past abuse. It's *never* the survivor's fault. I want to take a minute and let you digest that in case you're a survivor and have been blamed for what happened to you.

Maybe you've heard something like, "If you wouldn't have been wearing that, he would have left you alone." I might be the first one to say this to you, so you can read this as many times as you need to until it sinks in.

It. Was. Not. Your. Fault.

You are a daughter of God. I see you, love you, and want you to know you have value. It's OK if you need to put the book down after reading that and come back later when you're ready.

I believe we all have a deep desire to be seen—truly seen for who we are authentically. But the sad reality is that we live in a social media world where most people only post the best versions of themselves to try to be popular, get likes, and become IG famous. I get it. I've been guilty of this myself on more than one occasion. I've been so focused on what to post so I get new followers and, in the process, have lost sight of my vision, God's will, and my passion for creating meaningful content.

When you post on social media, you have the opportunity to get more than just likes; you can be a "social media influencer," a phrase that's been thrown around a lot lately, and it has me thinking. In what way do I want to be influencing my friends as well as possibly strangers? What's a mark I want to leave on the world? How do I want to be seen? Do people need to use the same makeup as me, buy my clothes, or obsess over my earrings? No. Not at all.

I know imitation is considered the highest form of flattery, but please, oh please, only imitate someone because you truly like what they wear, support, or believe in. Make sure your motivation is in the right place. I see so many people blindly following someone who compromises their core values in the hopes they will become popular by association.

Social media plays such a huge role in fashion trends. I know

I'm not the only person to follow accounts because I like the individual's style.

Yet, the way society (and social media) is defining and dictating modesty is worrisome. How are they defining it? They aren't. They're removing the standard all together. Want to walk around mostly naked? Go ahead.

Let's dissect and break down some of the common arguments against dressing modestly.

> By dressing to respect your body,
> you're actually oppressing yourself in some way or another.

That's a super big load of bull. Modesty has brought so much freedom to my life. I don't get hit on by gross men as often, I worry less about someone interpreting my intention incorrectly, and I don't have to feel like I'm being put on display for everyone to see and judge. I can be totally comfortable in my own skin.

> I can wear what I want and shouldn't have any consequences.

While I would love to say that we live in a safe world where all people are 100 percent good and have good intentions, it's just not true. We live in a sex-driven world right now. You can wear revealing clothing all you want, but if someone approaches you and tries to hit you up for a one-night stand, I wouldn't be surprised. Like one of my friends says, "If you dress like a prostitute, don't be offended when you get treated like one." Ouch, that hurts, but there also seems to be truth in that statement, right? I think back to the movie "Pretty Woman." Julia Roberts is a prostitute who gets hired to be a stand-in girlfriend of sorts for Richard Gere's character. A major scene in the movie is when Julia's character goes shopping for appropriate clothing to wear because everything she owns is short, tight, and revealing. That movie came out in 1990, and if you Google images of her prostitute outfits, they look very similar to fashion trends today. Please tell me I'm not the only one who is disturbed by this?

Being modest doesn't mean your closet has to look like your grandma's closet either. You can wear cute and trendy things while getting creative with the pairing of items. For example, wear a summer kimono over a tank or graphic tee and some longer shorts instead of wearing it over a crop top and booty shorts. Are those changes to the look cute? I think so. Do I care if others don't like it? Not really.

It's hard to do, but it's important to get to a point in your life where you don't need other people's approval. Like I mentioned at the beginning of the chapter, I want people to follow me for my meaningful content, not because they want to follow my style. If someone thinks I dress like a prude, I'm OK with that because at the end of the day, my actions are in line with my core values and that feels really good. It's me being authentic.

If my clothes are distracting to someone that's his/her problem not mine.

Yes, guys need to be held accountable for their actions. I believe that with my whole heart; however, I think we can play a big role in helping them make better choices. Let me explain.

A few years ago, I was watching Jessica Rey on YouTube talk about the evolution of the bikini. She spoke about a study done by Princeton University professors. The researchers wanted to know what parts of the brain were activated when male college students saw women dressed in a variety of clothing. They were shown women who were dressed modestly, and the medial prefrontal cortex lit up. That's the part of the brain that's stimulated when we're thinking about someone else's feelings or intentions. What the researchers found was astonishing to me.

They discovered that, when men saw women in bikinis or other minimally covering outfits, the part of the brain associated with tools, such as hammers and screw drivers, was activated, and for some of the men, their medial prefrontal cortex was not active at all. This means the men were reacting to the women as if they were not fully human. The men's brains were responding to those pictures the same way they would react to an inanimate object to be used.

As if that wasn't disturbing enough, in another study, the researchers also found that men who looked at women in bikinis associated with first person action verbs like "I push, I grab, I handle," but when they looked at women who were dressed more modestly they associated with third person action verbs like, "she pushes, she grabs, she handles.[1]" The reason this is terrifying to me is the fact that we, as women, want to have power. We want to have control over our lives and actions, but by dressing minimally, we're actually removing power from ourselves. We're encouraging men's brains to not see us as human beings.

Having this knowledge allows us to take back our power. We can wear items of clothing that cover more of our bodies, therefore, ensuring that the men we come in contact with will be interacting with us using the appropriate portion of their brains.

As women we have an obligation to respect the men in our lives. Whether that's our dads, grandpas, brothers, uncles, cousins, or best friends. I would never demand respect from someone if I wasn't willing to give it back to them in return. When women wear revealing clothing, it can cause our sweet brothers in Christ to stumble. As the study above mentioned, it can encourage men to look at us as an object to be used and not a person to be loved. It can encourage their brains to switch from seeing us as a beautiful sister in Christ to an object to lust over. That's such a harsh reality. Modesty isn't about covering up out of shame, it's about revealing our dignity. It's about encouraging men to live to a higher standard of respect for the women in their lives. We can't force them to respect us, but we sure can encourage them.

I have personally experienced more guys than I can count lusting after me and my body.

Maybe part of the reason you don't dress more modestly is because nobody ever told you it was acceptable. Maybe you don't feel super comfortable in your own skin, but you want to learn how to embrace your body and fight against the norms when they don't' align with your values. I'm not trying to sound dramatic when I say this, but the moment I started shopping for my body shape instead of shopping the latest trend, my self-love skyrocketed! There's a special magic that happens when you look at your body, identify the features you want to accentuate, and then find clothes that meet those needs.

I got so tired of trying to force my very tall, curvy frame into designs that simply weren't made for my body type. I embraced the fact that I'm unique. I grew to love my height (pun intended) and realized I have a body that is a blessing to me. I vowed to stop allowing clothing trends and designers to rob me of my joy. Seriously, trying to shop within the trends when you look like I do causes so much anxiety and feelings of worthlessness. I have some friends who can literally wear anything and look amazing, I don't criticize or put them down for their natural shape. Instead I encourage them to embrace their form, and I totally live vicariously through them and their amazing style!

Reflection

I want you to take a minute and think about what features you have that are unique. How can you celebrate your body and your dignity at the same time? Are you really short, long-legged, curvy, have small feet, or are you the "average woman" that clothing is designed for? Take some time to think about the features you like most about yourself. This isn't a time to hate on your body, but instead highlight what you like. For me, I love that I have an hourglass shape and can wear clothes that bring attention to my waist. I have green eyes and love to wear colors that bring out their brightness.

What areas of your body would you like to accentuate?

I think it's safe to say most of us can find at least one thing we love about our bodies. I can say with certainty that every single one of you reading this book could think of more things you don't like about your body, or parts of your body that you would be uncomfortable showing. When shopping for clothes, it's just as important to be mindful of these things so you can make choices you feel confident and comfortable in.

I'll give you an example. I have really long and curvy legs and a big ol' booty. If I buy short shorts, I'll take three steps and already have to tug and pull on them because they ride up. I like being present with people; therefore, I choose to buy longer shorts that stay in place so I can focus on the people I'm with instead of adjusting my shorts every five seconds. This is also an example of going against the fashion grain because we all know that short shorts are in style right now. If I can't find the shorts in a length I like, I'll just buy some cute summer dresses instead. Sometimes you just have to be like Ross Geller in the show *Friends* and yell, "Pivot!" to the original plan.

Let's take a second to jot down the parts of your body that cause anxiety or frustration when you're shopping. Knowing them ahead of time will help you identify what you need to look for and avoid the clothes you know won't work for you. Doing this mindfulness exercise has saved me so much time while shopping. I know what looks good on me now and don't have to have meltdowns in the dressing room anymore!

What parts of your body give you trouble? What clothing items have caused you to cry in the dressing room? What trends don't work for you and need to be avoided?

My bonus pro tip for shopping and maintaining modesty is to shop online if you can. Some stores offer longer lengths online, and you can try everything on in the comfort of your home. It allows you to have as much time as you need to look at the rest of your closet and see how the new item will work with your existing wardrobe. Most stores give you free return shipping or allow you to return to the store. This tip alone has saved me so many dressing-room tears.

Take Action

List your definition of modesty and how you will live by it.

Throw out any clothes that violate your personal modesty standard.

Are there any stores you will now avoid when going shopping? List them below.

Which stores will be your new go-to stores?

Take some time to go through your closet, item by item, and donate any apparel that doesn't align with your new modesty standards. Be encouraged, sweet sisters, you can totally learn to love yourself while having fun expressing your personal style and not violating your own boundaries.

7

When I'm Married I'll . . .

My Story

W hen I'm married, I'll . . . When I'm dating, I'll . . . When I have kids, I'll . . . When I retire, I'll . . . When I'm dead . . . well, then it will all be over.

Why are we constantly waiting for the next phase of life to happen before we start living? When I was in college, I had the high hopes of getting that Mrs. degree everyone talked about. I was excited to learn, but I was more excited about getting out of my small town, having new experiences, and of course, meeting my future husband. I can't tell you how many times people told me I would meet my husband at college. I know it happens for a lot of people, but I now laugh at the thought that it would be that easy. All I would have to do is show up to college, sit in some classes, hopefully pass those classes, and then, Bam! my magical husband would appear from the fairy godmother that I, of course, would have to have in order for this idea to become a reality.

I spent so much time wondering if the next guy I met would end up being my spouse that I kind of forgot to be present.

Looking back, I'm a little sad. Sad that I was so focused on finding love that it blinded me from partaking in some events. Or even worse, I went to events I didn't care about because "you aren't going to meet your husband sitting on your couch."

College was the beginning of my forced extroverted personality. I had such a fear of missing out on my future husband that it was causing a sense of panic. Like my time was ticking. Every day that went by where I wasn't in a relationship just felt like a failure.

For people who aren't in a relationship, a sense of failure can be magnified when all of their friends start seriously dating, getting engaged, and getting married. You may have the thought that you must be doing something wrong if you're single and they aren't. After all, you wanted a relationship just as badly as they did. What gave them the secret sauce that made it happen for them? That's when the shame starts setting in. Those deep, dark thoughts that only come out of shame from comparing ourselves to others. Thoughts like I'm not pretty enough, not thin enough, not interesting enough. What made him pick her over me? Am I invisible? I must be.

It's interesting what happens when a friend or family member finds out you're single. There are so many crazy responses I've heard like, "Oh honey, it's OK. He's out there somewhere." "One day you'll find him." "Keep your head up, you'll get married one day."

OK, fam, I said I was *single*, I'm not dying. Geez. I've noticed other people love to project their own personal desires onto us, with what I'm assuming are the best of intentions, but these intentions can be so shaming. Oh, hey, Aunt Susan, you don't want to hear about my thriving business, the work I do at my church, or the funny joke my friend told me. You just want to ask if I'm dating . . . OK. *Insert eye roll here.*

Now don't get me wrong. I'd love to be able to have a relationship to talk about, but since that's not what's happening in this phase of my life, how about we celebrate where I am? I know I said it at the beginning of the book, but I'll say it again for the cheap seats in the back. Being single is an amazing privilege!

Crazy thought, right?

Since we're going with the thought that all the family comments come from good intentions, let's go ahead and assume they also might be coming from a place of ignorance. I've found it can be helpful to educate your family members on the phase of life you're in. You don't have to apologize for loving your job, your friends, your apartment, pets, volunteer work, etc. You don't have to apologize for being happy right where you are. When your family asks if you're dating, you can say no, and then be excited about what else is happening in your life. It's OK to be excited. It's alright to want to share that excitement with the people around you.

Let me warn you, though, some of your family won't care what you're doing outside of your relationship status, and they won't care to engage in any other conversation with you. I want you to know that type of behavior from your family members or friends is most likely not about you but is coming from their own insecurities. There's no need for you to feel shame about your current relationship status.

When it comes to family gatherings and social engagements, it's so important to know what your boundaries are so you can enforce them and allow people to respect them. Remember, you do not owe anyone the details of your personal journey. What I mean by that is this: I only engage in conversation with other individuals who are going to celebrate my accomplishments, cheer me on, or give me constructive feedback when needed. I give very vague details to the people that will rain on my parade simply because misery loves company.

Throughout this dating season of your life, you may find it challenging to find people who want to show up for you and support you. These types of people are the kind who say things out of love and with the best intentions. Not those who can't give you feedback without shaming you. Your challenge when setting boundaries is to let go of the people who want to pull you down and run toward the friends that want to build you up.

Reflection

It can be challenging to thrive in your single phase of life when you feel the need to justify why you are single. Before we dive deeper into growing your passions, I want you to feel more comfortable acknowledging where you are in life, right here, right now.

What are the best things happening in your life right now? (e.g., your job is awesome, you have amazing friends, you sold a piece of your artwork, you're training for a marathon)

What do you appreciate most about being single?

Is there something you are doing right now, that wouldn't be as easy or even possible if you were in a serious relationship or married?

Take Action

It's no secret that it's easy to get into a funk from time to time when we are single. We can't be positive Patty's about it all the time. When you are feeling stuck in a negative mindset, I want you to redirect your focus. This could look like a lot of different things, so I'll give you a few examples to get you started, but feel free to make this process your own.

Step 1. Turn back to your reflection on the previous page and acknowledge all you have accomplished. Spend some time being grateful for your ability to do whatever you are desiring at the moment. Make a list of ten things you are thankful for, then choose one item you want to focus on (e.g., I love running and I'm thankful for a body that allows me to run, so I'm going to exercise today and feel joy that I can move my body in this way).

Step 2. Nurture a friendship. Do not, I repeat, do not isolate yourself when you are feeling down. Isolation grows shame, insecurity, and negativity. Instead, go get coffee with a friend; go to a baseball game, a movie, dinner, or bowling alley; or take a walk together. Get out of your house and out of your head. Lean into the people who want to speak life into you.

Step 3. Make a list of the people close to you who aren't supportive of your single life and avoid them if you aren't feeling good about where your life is at the moment.

You, dear friend, are not invisible. You have a life that's worth living, one that has so much potential to be amazing and everything that you want it to be! Do not, I repeat, *do not* put your life on hold. There's no part of your life that is promised to you, so make the most of what you have every single day!

8

Igniting Your Passions

My Story

Sometimes it can take a lot of exploring to find your passions and joys. When you find a passion, it feels like something you were born with. It touches a part of your soul you didn't even know was reachable. A few years ago, I realized I was putting my life on hold, waiting for my significant other to be by my side before exploring my passions. I thought I needed that other person around to validate how I was spending my time. I got tired of that and decided to step outside my comfort zone and not let fear stop me from chasing adventure.

Traveling was one of those things I had put on hold. Since I was already twenty-six and had not been on a plane yet, I figured I might as well wait to take my first trip with my future husband because it sounded romantic and picturesque. But all I got from waiting was a lack of experience, adventure, and fun.

My friend Brandon really pushed me into adventure and met me at the end of my first solo flight to Las Vegas. I give him quite a bit of the credit for helping me realize I can do things in life twice. I could take a trip to San Diego on a fun girl's trip and still go again and share those experiences with my spouse down the road if I chose to.

I realized I was stuck in these mental traps. Lies that I had made up and told myself or heard from someone else. "Do not go to that place alone; it will ruin the whole trip. Wait for the right person to go with you. You want to make memories with your special someone!" Why have I spent my whole adult life with this mindset? I'm so glad Brandon came along when he did and helped me to realize that other people in my life also hold a great deal of value.

There are challenges that come from starting to live a life of passion and purpose. It was definitely overwhelming to me at first and I didn't know where to get started. So, I'm going to give you a view into my life and hope my experiences will inspire a starting point.

I'm very passionate about being an authentic person. It's hard to put into words the joy I get from being a friend, daughter, sister friend, and Auntie Kissa to my countless adopted nieces and nephews. When I was eighteen, I was a scared little naïve girl who moved to a college seven hours away from home. I knew I needed to find a community in that new town and then again when I moved two years later. My adopted family, or framily, as I call them, totally changed my life. I cannot count how many framily members have welcomed me into their homes over holidays and birthdays when I was not able to see my own family. All of these relationships truly fill up my love cup. It took me longer than I'd like to admit, but these roles I play in other people's lives are a huge part of my life's purpose.

My love of flying is like nothing I've ever felt before. My first flight was from Dallas to a work conference in Las Vegas. I got dropped off at the airport by a friend who reassured me I would be OK (thanks, Bailey!), made my way through security, found my gate, and finally started breathing again. I was so nervous. After an hour-and-half-long delay after boarding, we were off! I was terrified to get into a plane the first time. Experiencing that first take-off filled me with panic and excitement, which most of the time feel very similar to me.

Everything about this first landing was thrilling, though: the sounds and sights of coming into a new city, the feeling of gliding gently to the ground. In true Vegas fashion, I arrived just after midnight. By the time I got there, I could hardly remember our delayed flight and everyone's frustration. The overall positive experience completely overpowered those minor negative details. As soon as I came home from my first trip, I could not wait to get myself back on a plane again.

Traveling anywhere, whether it be via road trip or a flight, hits my soul in a similar way to my first flight. Going to a new place, meeting new people, seeing new things, eating new food, and breathing in different air reignites my faith. It's so rejuvenating to my soul! It helps me slow down and appreciate sights and sounds I wouldn't normally notice during my typical fast-paced life. During those moments, I appreciate God's beauty on a different level.

I also especially love traveling to the beach—any beach that has nice sand for me to squish my toes in. The waves soothe me. The people-watching never seems to disappoint, and you can usually find the best greasy foods at little hole-in-the-wall places nearby. I have yet to travel to a beach that didn't have this effect on me. You may be wondering why I'm deeply describing my beach love affair, but I want to paint a big, bright picture for you. I want you to be able to have passions in your life that affect you in an extremely positive way.

If I had stuck with my narrow mindset, I may never have

learned how much I love to travel. Sometimes taking risks pays off!

Those are some example of my big passions. Now, let's talk about some of the fun little things in life. It's the simple things that bring me great fulfillment on a daily basis.

Traveling is great but it's not possible to do that frequently enough to give me the level of fulfillment I desire in my day-to-day life. I can argue that I'm equally as passionate about these daily passions as I am the big passions.

What are some of my simple joys? A good cup of coffee or chai tea latte gives me life. I'm on a first name basis with a barista at my favorite local coffee shop. Seriously. Johnny is the best. He's been my ride-or-die coffee creator for the last three years and counting.

Mixing new cocktails and cooking new recipes is a place for me to get adventurous in different ways and it also brings my friends together because it's not as much fun to cook or drink alone.

I'm a huge fan of taking care of my body. I have been getting weekly massages for the last year and half. I was never so aware of how I carry my stress until I started taking care of myself. Working out several times a week also gives me a place to release my stress.

Now, I would not go so far as to say that exercising is a passion because most days, I don't want to do it. I am, by nature, a sloth; however, I have a passion for taking care of the one body God blessed me with. Group dance classes are the only workout I actually truly like and shaking my hips with some friends will always make me giggle.

I love feeling connected to my tribe on a regular basis, which is why I keep my friend circle close and meet people wherever I go. Just because you aren't in a romantic relationship, doesn't mean you can't have hobbies and enjoy a super-rich, full life.

In the interest of full disclosure, I have to tell you that I'm actually sitting in a coffee shop in California while I write this chapter. I've had a chai tea latte. I spent a large part of yesterday morning at the beach. Spent time walking around the Redondo Pier. Watched seals (ocean puppies as I call them.) Hung out with my mom who came on this trip with me. I ran into the freezing ocean even though it's cloudy and about 60 degrees. (I still can't feel my toes in case you are wondering.) We just all-around had a blast exploring. This trip encompassed so many of my passions and I felt like it was important to give you a real-life, in-the-moment example of how I'm embracing life fulfillment.

Through my journey of finding my passions, I've learned that self-love is a big part of that journey. You have to believe you're worthy of living a full life before you can start living it out. For years, I was punishing myself for not being in a relationship. Acting as if some things were off limits to me until I had a significant other to share them with.

Once I realized I was worthy of positive experiences, I started to allow myself to have them. I quickly found out that weekly massages are life-giving. This may sound silly, but as a person who thrives on physical touch, getting a massage once a week was something that kept me from jumping into relationships just to get some physical contact with someone. Having a tribe of women who love hugs also helped satisfy my physical touch needs, as well as letting my nieces and nephews treat me like a human jungle gym.

I'm very active in my church. It's the place I've found my steady tribe of friends and framily. Going to church on Sundays is what gets me through the week. If I'm sick and miss, my week just doesn't feel the same. On the first night of teaching religion class, one of my small group girls came right out and asked, "So why are you single?" My co-leader couldn't hide her laugh at the boldness of that question. It was truly a joy to be able to talk about how my faith guides my life, including my spiritual life. It's funny how God can take little moments and turn them into an affirming conversation that I personally needed to hear again.

I hope this chapter challenges you to find your passions, or to begin living them out again if they fell to the back burner. It you want to live a full life; you must be intentional with how you spend your time and who you spend your time with.

Jim Rohn famously said we are the average of the five people we spend the most time with. When you think of your passions, are you spending time with people who want to support your adventures? Are you around friends who want to see you have fun and fulfillment? You now know you're allowed to have fun, friends, and framily. Let's talk about being intentional with your time. Answer the next few questions to help you see if you're in the right place with the right people.

Reflection

Who are your five closest friends?

1.

2.

3.

4.

5.

On a scale of one–ten, how fulfilled are you right now? (circle a number)

1 2 3 4 5 6 7 8 9 10

How often do you take time to have fun or try something new? (Circle one.)

1. Never
2. Couple of times a month
3. Once/twice a week
4. Several times a week
5. Daily/multiple times a day

What's an action that you are going to take to be more intentional with your time?

Use the answers to this quiz as a way of showing yourself who you are now, and from this point on, make an intentional effort to not be mediocre.

Take Action

What are some things you've been wanting to do, try, or experience that you've been putting off?

Make a commitment to try one new thing a week for ten weeks. You can do things alone or with a friend. The purpose is to put yourself out there and not let the fear of the unknown keep you from living your best life. Write down your new adventure plans below!

Week 1:

Week 2:

Week 3:

Week 4:

Week 5:

Week 6:

Week 7:

Week 8:

Week 9:

Week 10:

Having a hard time thinking of new things? Feeling a bit stuck? Feel free to steal some examples below.

- Try a new coffee shop or restaurant
- Go to a movie alone for the first time
- Get concert tickets for your favorite band
- Rent a kayak and spend a day on the water
- Pack a picnic and your favorite book and head to a park for the day
- Go Skydiving
- Take a solo trip somewhere

- Road trip for a day
- Challenge yourself to smile at ten people every day for a week
- Go on a hike or camping weekend
- Learn to surf, paddle board, or water ski
- Rock climb
- Read a whole book in a day
- Say hello to the guy you've been making googly eyes at
- Cook a three course meal from scratch
- Give up social media for a week

I want to know what you tried! When you start your adventures, make sure you share on IG and tag me! @Clarissa_christensen I can't wait to see how your lives are going to change in ten weeks. So much adventure is waiting for you!

Disclaimer: The author is not liable for any injuries or damages acquired while being adventurous and/or finding your passions. Try new things at your own risk.

9

Finding Your Tribe

My Story

So many women (and men) go on dates with the wrong people and stay in unhealthy relationships out of loneliness. Often, loneliness comes mainly from the lack of a support system. I'm talking about the people who don't have strong family ties or maybe don't have that many, if any, friends. So, let's talk about how to find your tribe!

Why are solid friendships important? Oh geez, where do I even start? Our nourishing friendships can lead us down a path that's encouraging, loving, supportive, and joyful overall. But destructive friendships can lead you to a dark place filled with insecurities, sadness, anxiety, and stress. I think we can all agree we'd choose the first set of qualities.

It's totally possible to have positive, healthy friendships, ones that hold you accountable to your life goals, whether they're mental, physical, spiritual, academic, occupational, or so on. Your true friends have your best interests at heart. For example, if your friend knows you're trying to get an academic scholarship for college, she probably isn't going to support you partying the night before your SAT. In other words, she's not going to encourage you to blow off the things in life that are important to you.

In order to find healthy friends, I recommend you set your friendship standards high, like your dating standards, and think of them as being long-term, like your romantic relationships. You don't want to emotionally invest in someone who'll kick you to the curb the first chance they get.

One of my best friends I've known since eighth grade and another I met eleven years ago. They're currently my two longest-lasting relationships. The reason these friendships have lasted so long is because they're built on a foundation of our faith. We all want good things for each other and call each other out when we need to.

How can you encourage lasting friendships in your life? Find people you connect with over common goals, interests, and/or core values. For instance, I've met most of my friends at church. We have a common goal of helping each other get to heaven. We all want to live a life that's pleasing to God and live in a way that serves him. We're all constantly trying to follow God's will and spend time encouraging each other and building each other up when times get hard. I've had "friends" who've encouraged me to abandon my faith when I'm walking through a hard time, and friends—let me tell you —as someone who is very connected to my spiritual life, abandoning it was the opposite of what I needed. That was an eye-opener to me. It helped me to see which friends I can pull closer and be more vulnerable with and which ones need to stay at arm's length.

This brings me to an important point. Not everyone is going to be your friend. I don't care how nice you are, whether you make the best chocolate chip cookies ever or know the best coffee shops around. There will always be people around you who can't see past their own insecurities to see your worth. This is a hard lesson for most of us to learn.

Raise your hand if you're a people pleaser! *silently raises hand* Let me tell ya, it's exhausting chasing down friendships and trying to win people over. My friendships now take minimal effort. Trying to coordinate five schedules for a girl's night is basically the only challenge we have. I love my Friday night girls. We make tacos, drink wine, and chat about life. They've seen me at my best and my worst and love me no matter what I'm going through.

If you're in friendships where the other person rarely supports you, puts you down frequently, makes you work for their attention, or punishes you when you unintentionally hurt their feelings, then you're not in a healthy friendship. Run, just run away.

Please, please, please, do not chase friendships with people who don't realize what you have to offer. Run toward the friends who are running toward you! Here's your reminder with my all-time favorite quote. "Rejection is God's protection.[1]" Can you hear me when I say this? People that want you in their life are going to make time for you and let you know how important you are to them and how much they value you. Allow the people who are constantly walking away from you to leave.

When I was in grad school, I was so busy. Like all-the-time busy, barely-made-it-out-alive busy. My best friend made it a point to reach out to me almost daily. She would check in, see how things were going, and allow me to fall apart. I was definitely taking more from the friendship than I was putting into it. I would frequently tell her how much I loved our friendship, how bad I felt that I hardly reached out first, and how much I valued her taking the lead during this time in my life when I was barely keeping my head above water. Then when she went to grad school, I had the privilege of taking the lead and checking in on her and letting her know I was cheering her on and supporting her in whatever way I could. You guys, this is friendship. It's not 50/50, give and take, push and pull all the time. It's being able to say, "Hey, I see you have a lot of burdens. Let me help you with that," and knowing they will do the same for you when you need it. It doesn't work if one person is *always* doing all the work. God calls us to love one another and take care of each other, but he does not call us to be used and abused by others.

Now that you know what qualities to look for, let's talk about where you might meet some new friends.

If you're in college, chat with the people around you. I didn't make a ton of lasting friends within my degree plan, but it sure made my college experience much nicer to have study partners and lots of help if I missed a day of class. You can also join sororities if you have the time and funds. Most campuses have a variety of Bible study and spirituality groups to meet the needs of whatever faith you practice.

What about if you're out of college or in a new place starting your career? It gets ten thousand times harder to meet people after college. My best advice is to find hobbies that involve other people. If you meet someone while participating in an activity you both enjoy, you'll already have a common connection and that can be a starting point to conversing, which can be a great way to get to know people on a deeper level.

Some examples would be taking any kind of workshop or class like painting, cooking, hand lettering, dancing, and gardening. There are a ton of classes to take offered by locally owned establishments or community colleges. Joining local online social media groups can also help connect you to other people. You can join fitness classes or try rock climbing or Pilates. Find a place of worship and get involved in any of their young adult activities or singles mixers. Volunteer in some capacity, join a Bible study, go on a retreat, or attend potlucks or fellowship events.

Another way to meet like-minded individuals is to join networking groups. Connecting with other professionals can be great for your business but also creates a space for friendships to grow.

I met one of my best friends in a fitness class. I never thought I would gain a sister simply from going to work out, but it happened. How did it happen? I noticed she had a hole in her pants and didn't want her walking around all day being exposed. So I pointed it out, and the rest is history!

Workout classes tend to be extremely encouraging and positive places, so the next time you go to the gym, take a class instead of a solo workout. Or maybe pull your headphones out of your ears and engage with anyone around you.

No matter what option you choose, always remember to stay open-minded. You never know who you might meet when you're open to connection. This type of openness can lead to friendships and maybe even the romantic relationships you're desiring as well. Remember, you have so much worth as an individual, there is no need to hide in fear. You are worthy of being seen!

Before we conclude this chapter, I want to share different perspectives on where to find friends. I went to social media and asked the following questions.

Question 1: How/where did you meet your current friend group?

- Connecting through social media
- Conferences
- Work training
- School
- Work
- Church Retreats
- Yoga
- Coffee shops
- Book clubs
- Fitness classes

Question 2: What are your hobbies?

- Reading
- Yoga
- Traveling
- Going to the gym
- Going to the dog park
- Walking my dog
- Hiking
- Cycling
- Cooking
- Hosting social events

You guys, there are **so** many fun options! I encourage you to try something new if you're feeling like you're stuck in a rut.

I want you to get a good idea of where you believe you stand with your current friends. Take the friendship quiz below and reach out to me if you need help!

Reflection

1. How many healthy relationships do you currently have? List them by name below.

2. If your answer is zero healthy relationships, what's one new activity you want to try this week to put yourself out there? Answer below.

3. Who are some "friends" you need to let go of and stop chasing? List below.

4. Do you feel paralyzed by the fear of taking an action? Are you alone and don't know what your next move is? Do you think you need some personal attention to help grow your confidence in building your tribe?

Yes_____ No_____

Take Action

If you answered yes to most or all of those questions in your reflection, visit my website and set up a one-on-one coaching session with me to help break down the barriers and move you into a thriving life filled with amazing friendships. www.igniteyourworth.com.

Do you already have some great friends you are connected to? Have you been making excuses as to why you can't see them more often? Your challenge is to nurture those friendships. I want you to focus on spending time with at least one friend a week. Make sure your time together is in person. You can also video chat if it's a long distant friendship. To take the challenge a step further, commit to turning your phone off for the duration of your time together. Really focus on being present with your friends.

If you are feeling alone and needing to connect with an awesome community of supportive women, I encourage you to join my Facebook group. I'd love to chat with you and introduce you to some amazing friends. Facebook.com/groups/igniteyourworth

10

The Pink Elephant in the Room: Discernment

L et's rip the Band-Aid off and say it. Some of you reading this book will not get married or have any type of committed long-term relationship. You simply won't. I know that sounds harsh, but sometimes the truth hurts.

Why did I just verbally punch you in the face, you might ask? One of my pet peeves when talking to other people about *my* dating life is the steadfast assurance that I *will* "find the one," because my "Prince Charming" is out there somewhere.

Well I hate to be the bearer of bad news, but we are not all called to be married. This idea might be a shock to some of you. Since we were old enough to watch princess movies, we've been fed the idea of the fairytale life that, of course, includes a Prince Charming. Have you noticed those movies always end with the prince and princess getting married? Unlike the movies, a wedding is not where your story ends, especially if some of you are not called to the vocation of marriage.

Many of you might be called to a nontraditional life. Maybe

you have no desire to get married, but you're reading this book hoping to figure out what's wrong with you because you want to devote your life to your career. Or how about those of you who are feeling called to the religious life, but your mom is so set on you getting married and having children that your head feels fuzzy about all of it?

It is so important to spend time discerning what your calling is. For a lot of you, your calling will be career, family, and kids, or some combination of the three. Some of you might be in the percentage of people who are called to a religious life, which is why I believe it's extremely important to spend time discerning.

Clients often ask me "How do I discern? How do I know what path is for me? How can I tell God's will from what I want for my life? What if the two are different?" Those are all great questions. God uses so many different ways to communicate his will to us. I wish there was a cookie-cutter answer to all of those questions. One thing I can say for certain, you can never go wrong with prayer and meditation as a place to start.

I have included my top seven tips for discerning your vocation. Fun fact, I have done all of these at some point and time in my life and found them to be very helpful.

Discernment tips:

1. Keep a prayer/meditation journal.

I'm a fan of having a prayer journal. You can write down your intentions, reflect on them, put the date at the top of the page, and witness how much your life changes. Over time, you'll be able to see how much you have grown. It can also allow you the space to write down all of God's blessings in your life. Gratitude journals can help you see all the things you currently have and not fixate so much on what you don't.

. . .

2. Get a spiritual director.

This component of discernment has been huge for some of my friends. It has really helped hold them accountable to their spiritual beliefs, which made it easier to not settle for a partner who was living outside of their standards. A spiritual director can also help you grow your faith and develop your relationship with the Lord. As I mentioned earlier, this was a big void in my own life I was trying to fill.

3. Have friends you trust.

This feels like a duh statement, but I never cease to be amazed at the number of people I meet who don't have friends at all or who don't have friends whose values align with their own. This is extremely important because peer pressure is a real thing. If your thoughts about relationships differ from everyone else in your social circle, you may find yourself at a crossroads of wanting to forget about your dating goals and instead, follow the crowd. Some of you may have friends who will support you even if they don't understand your dating goals and that's great! Please don't think I am encouraging you to shut out lifelong friends, that's not the point. The point I want to drive home is the need for a positive and encouraging support system to back you up in this phase of life. I pray you have that network, and if you don't, that you're able to cultivate those relationships soon!

4. Prayer and meditation.

It is so important to spend time in prayer and meditation when you're discerning. I would like to stress the importance of having some quiet time alone. It can be a challenge to hear God's voice when you're constantly distracted by music, Netflix, and friends. Silence is also a place to truly test yourself to see how secure you are at being alone. A lot of you can't handle the thoughts in your head. Scary thoughts can come from isolation. If you stay busy and distracted all the time out of fear of your thoughts, I encourage you to go to counseling so you can identify what's causing those thoughts and gain healing. My favorite place to find quiet time is at my church's chapel or while lying in bed at the beginning of the day.

5. Be specific.

When you're praying, journaling, and reflecting on your vocation, be specific in the way you ask God to reveal himself to you. When I was discerning my vocation, I told God I wanted to receive a bouquet of flowers as a sign of confirmation that I would be married one day. I am fully aware that I can tell God what I want all day long and it doesn't mean he'll deliver the answer to my prayers in the exact way I asked. But, in this case, he did. I definitely cried when that bouquet came to my office one day. I was very intentional with my prayers and with my request for flowers. You see, I've only received flowers once in my life from an ex-boyfriend, so I knew this would be a good way to know he was speaking to me. I would never ask for a prayer confirmation through something that was a common occurrence in my life. That merely opens the door for confusion and frustration.

6. Have married friends.

Maybe you feel like you're constantly surrounded by your married friends who are mushy in love. It can get frustrating to feel like you're the odd man out, but I encourage you to embrace any opportunity you have to get to know some older married couples. The ones who are out of the honeymoon stage and will be able to be real with you about their marriage. It has been so helpful to hear my friends talk about and see firsthand what it's like to be married. The good, the bad, and everything in between. If you're not sure whether you want kids, hang out with your friends' kids and see if your desire to have them grows or goes away.

7. Shadow the vocation.

You could be called to many different vocations. The most obvious one we think about is marriage and family life. Many people overlook the religious life. In that vocation, you could be called to a number of organizations: the priesthood, missionary work, a convent, a monastery, or pastoring a church, to name a few. If you're feeling drawn to a religious vocation or mission field, take the time to get to know someone living out that vocation. It's a great idea to spend a day in the life of someone who had chosen to stay single. You can ask them about their life fulfillment and how they came to the conclusion that the single life was for them. I would suggest the same if you are discerning marriage and children as well. You can walk a mile in a stay-at-home mom's shoes by offering to keep her kids for the day. Remember, the best way to rule out a vocation is to know the ins and outs of the lifestyle.

As I mentioned earlier, I was homeschooled from kindergarten through my senior year of high school. During that time, my family was part of a Catholic homeschool group and one of our annual field trips was a visit to a local convent every February. We would take valentines to the nuns, put on a talent show, and have conversations and refreshments with them. (As I type that, I can't help but think, "Wow. It doesn't get more Catholic than that.")

In addition to our annual trips, each student also "adopted a nun" to be our pen pal. We would write letters back and forth, exchange birthday cards, and go visit them as often as we could. Through that experience, God revealed the beauty of the religious life to me. He also showed me the religious life was not for me. It's hard to explain how I received that confirmation, but somehow, I knew that's not where God wanted me. Our God is a God of peace. He doesn't want to stir up anxiety and worry, and my heart wasn't settled in the convent. I loved visiting my friends there, but at the same time, I felt like I would suffocate if I stayed too long.

The thought of discerning your vocation may seem scary at first. This is an incredibly vulnerable step to take in your single life. You may find yourself afraid of what the answer is. What if you get the answer but it's followed by a lot of waiting? God confirmed my vocation the first time when I was nineteen, then again when I was twenty-three. When I was twenty-seven and still not married, I prayed more, and he confirmed my vocation yet again. As I sit here writing this, I'm twenty-nine, still unmarried, without children, yet I still feel called to the vocation of marriage and family.

Knowing your vocation so far ahead of time can give you a bag of conflicting emotions. I weave in and out of excitement, frustration, and "what the heck is happening?" But I realized the not-so-happy emotions were coming from my lack of trust in God's plan. Trust. Remember that word we mentioned at the beginning of the book? Yep, it comes up daily in my life and especially in the area of my love life. I remind myself daily that I have to trust the bigger plan. God has a plan. He's had it since the day I was born, so why am I stressing out about how the chapters of my love story unfold?

People stress for a lot of reasons, but a huge one is fear of judgment, fear that our family and friends would view us as "less than" because of certain decisions we make. Personally, I feel like I'm walking a hard line sometimes between fully embracing my career and the blessing of the moment, while trying not to forget to pray for my future. But when thoughts like this infiltrate your mind and cause you stress, it's important to remind yourself that it's perfectly fine to live in the present while praying for the future.

Reflection

Have you ever discerned your vocation? Yes_____ No_____

Do you feel a connection to one vocation more than the others?

Was there a discernment step that stuck out to your more than the others? Yes_____ No_____

If yes, which one?

Take a minute and think about what feelings you had while reading this chapter. Did you have a burning desire to be a wife and a mother? Did you give yourself permission to run toward your career? Was the idea of joining a religious order sounding more appealing? Write down whatever your initial reactions were to the discernment steps.

Take Action

I want you to pick the discernment step you connected with the most and focus on that one step for a month. Be intentional with the action you take around it. For example, if you decide to start a prayer journal, take time to pray and journal daily. If you choose to seek spiritual direction, don't just go once, but rather, attend several sessions. Dedicate time daily to these efforts and you will surely bear fruit.

11

Praying for Your Future Spouse

My Story

I was nineteen years old the first time I remember anyone talking to me about praying for my future spouse. My friend Jolene and I were talking about the current guy that I was kinda-sorta-maybe dating. He was the Bible study boy I mentioned previously. As I was sharing about our hang-outs (they weren't really dates), she challenged me to pray for my future spouse and to ask God what he wanted for my life and for my spouse.

I had heard about other people praying for their spouses, but it wasn't an idea I could easily comprehend at the time. I always prayed for people that I knew or for someone's family member. I don't think I had ever really made the connection that you could pray for someone you didn't know yet. But on December 28, 2018, I decided that praying for my future spouse in my daily prayer life was something I needed to do if I was going to be able to hear God speak to that part of my life.

I guess you could say I set a spiritual new year's resolution. If I wanted my future marriage to be built on a foundation of God, then why not start building that foundation now? I thought that if I could get in the habit of praying for him before we were ever together, then praying for him would be easier once we started our relationship and he actually had a face and a name. But I encountered some challenges while praying for him.

I never realized how much time I was going to spend thinking and dreaming about this man—like actually dreaming about my wedding, my future kids, the house we would live in. Night after night, I would fall asleep and have future-husband dreams. I thought I would be able to say a prayer for him in the morning and then go on about my day without a second thought given to him. Well, that wasn't the case.

I was (and still am) praying over different aspects of his life that I want protection over. I prayed for his strength, wisdom, and courage to name a few. In doing so, that led to a lot of thoughts about what his strength in character might look like. In what type of situation might he have to exercise courage? Would he be defending someone or standing up for a social injustice? You see where I'm going with this?

I got sucked into a rabbit hole of thoughts that began to consume me. The positive side was that every single time I thought about him, I would pray for him. Whoever he is out there, he's gotten a lot of spiritual love from me so far!

Bottom line: When you pray for your future spouse, know that you might have him on your mind frequently as a result. If you can prepare yourself for that, having your future spouse on your mind throughout the day doesn't have to be a bad thing at all. If you're able to pray for him more, it can help your day-to-day discernment.

I don't have any specific prayers to give you because it's my belief that we're all different; therefore, how we need to pray is unique. What I will tell you is this: think about that non-nego-tiable list you made earlier in the book. (If you haven't done it yet, hit pause, go make the list, and come back.)

Ok, so thinking about that list you made, what qualities and characteristics did you write down? Speak life into those! For instance, if you want someone who is rooted in his faith, is a provider, and a has good relationships with his family members, your prayer could look something like this,

"God, I ask that you be close to my future husband today. I pray he is able to feel your presence and draws closer to you no matter his circumstances. I ask that you be faithful to him in his efforts to keep a job and instill in him a strong work ethic. I ask that he has an awareness of his finances and is a good steward of his money. I pray you heal any wounds he has with his family and pray they are able to grow in love with one another. I ask you would protect his purity and shield him against sexual sin and a pornography addiction. It's in your name I pray. Amen."

Again, that's just an example of how I pray for my future husband. If that seems inauthentic to you, make it your own. You may have totally different prayer intentions, and that's alright. I highly recommend you ask God to protect your future husband from a pornography addiction or help heal him from one he may already have. A great many men and women are addicted to porn, so out of all the prayers to pray, that's one I would 100 percent recommend praying daily.

As you pray for your future spouse, I want you to also pray for yourself too. I think it's extremely easy for us to focus only on the other person, especially when we hear things from our family and friends like, "God hasn't finished working on your husband yet."

But what about us, sweet sisters? God surely has not perfected us, nor will we ever be perfect. That realization hit me like a ton of bricks one day. My literal thought was, "OMG! What if I'm not married yet because *I'm* the one who needs more work? What if my sweet husband already has all the qualities I've been praying for, and God's waiting on me to grow into the type of wife and mother my husband needs?" Boom, mic drop. Done.

Friends, we have to pray for ourselves. It's not selfish. It's actually arrogant *not to* pray for ourselves. We must have humble hearts that can admit we don't have all the answers. We have to know that we mess up a lot and need to extend grace to ourselves. The better we are at practicing grace and forgiveness with ourselves, the more automatic it will be to do so with our future husbands. From what all my married friends tell me, grace and forgiveness is absolutely necessary when you're married.

How do you want to pray over your spouse? You can write down your prayer below.

Reflection

Let's get to practicing! I pray daily that I can grow into the wife that my future husband deserves to have in his life. If I'm praying daily for God to bless me with a good man, then I need to be a good woman standing beside him. I challenge you to pray and ask God what needs to be changed in your hearts.

- What are the ugly parts of your life that need more Jesus?
- Do you complain a lot?
- Are you judgmental?
- Do you have a hard time staying away from gossip?
- Do you have a solid faith?
- Are you loving and patient?
- Do you need healing from an addiction?

Spend some time reflecting and asking God how he would like to work in your heart during your single life. Write down your thoughts and prayers on this page so you can flip back to it and pray over your own life daily.

Spend some time reflecting and asking God how he would like to work in your heart during your single life. Write down your thoughts and prayers on this page so you can flip back to it and pray over your own life daily.

Take Action

Now that you've spent some time reflecting on all the inner most parts of your heart, write down a prayer that you would like to pray over yourself daily.

Prayer to be a happy, healthy wife.

Now write down a daily prayer for your future spouse.

Now commit to saying these prayers daily.

12

The Men Who Guide Me

My Story

I feel like I can't talk about my dating journey and discernment without taking the time to give credit to so many of the influential men in my life who have helped me cultivate the standards I have in place for my future husband.

From the time I was a wee little girl, my dad has been a shining light in my life. He's kind, caring, honest, loving, and the most trustworthy guy I know. I grew up watching the way that he treated my mom, my sister, and myself. He opened doors for us, helped us out with homework (sometimes with a tearful ending because . . . math is hard) and has always supported my passions. I have always wanted a husband who is just as hardworking as my dad. He would work his regular job, take care of the land and animals we had, and still make time to come to any events we had. He would be my sound equipment guy when I competed in voice competitions, often-times accompanying me with his guitar and vocals. He donates his time to his church and has a true servant heart. He spent a lot of time with me playing gin rummy and singing while I was growing up and helped establish the foundation of what I like to call my "man standard."

My Gramps and Paw-Paw had a similar influence on my life. They possess so many of the same qualities as my dad. It's obvious that my dad was raised by my Paw-Paw and that my mom chose a man who was like her father in so many of the best ways. Both of my grandpas are Godly men who treat everyone with respect and are a joy to be round. They truly are / were men who valued quality time with their families. The older I get, the more I have come to realize how much the relationships we have in our younger years can impact us as adults. My Paw-Paw passed away four years ago and I still miss him, but the memories we made together are etched on my heart. I am forever grateful for all the examples he set for me. My Gramps is still independent at age ninety and continues to be a strong leader of our family. He prays for us daily, probably multiple times a day, and always has a five-dollar bill in his pocket to "tip the cook" when we make a meal for him. I also blame him for my chocolate addiction since he always had a stash readily available to us.

My friend Chris and I met when we were in eighth grade. Both homeschooled and pretty awkward at the time, we became long-distance friends who only saw each other a couple of times a year. Competing in an English class our senior year of high school turned us into best friends, though. (It's important to note here that I made a better grade than he did in the course. Sorry, Chris.) If you've never had a best friend of the opposite sex, you're missing out!

Chris was my go-to in college for all things guy-related. I would talk to him about guys I liked, and he would give me his honest advice or opinion of them. He was there when everything fell apart with my ex and helped me put the pieces back together.

On the flip side, I was someone who encouraged him to ask his now wife on their first date. To give you some insight into Chris's character, he is so much like my dad. He's a good, hardworking, Christian gentleman. You should be starting to see a trend with the men in my life. While in high school, if a guy liked me, I would always ask myself, "Does he treat me as well as Chris?" If the answer was no, I would move along.

I had so much respect for him that he greatly contributed to the standard for any guy I dated. Which is probably why I never dated anyone in high school. There was nobody around who could come close to treating me as well as he did.

I owe a lot to that friendship. I truly believe knowing Chris saved me from so much heartache. Even when my self-esteem was at its worst, Chris helped me realize my worth. I would frequently reflect on the fact that if he took the time to be so kind and caring to me as my friend, then any and all potential suiters would have to be on or above his level of respect for me. He was more mature than most guys his age, which I believe is partly why he treated everyone with the respect and dignity they deserved. I am happy to say he and I are still friends, and it has been an incredible blessing to watch him grow into the amazing husband and father he is today.

You know how I mentioned my Friday night tribe? Well, let me tell you about their husbands. I love the saying, "behind every good man is a good woman." So, I guess that means, "In front of every good woman is a good man." It's so true in the case of my Friday night friends. Their husbands are awesome! Even though I've only known them for three years, they've quickly grown to be special men in my life. They lead their families fearlessly with love and support for their wives and children. It's so obvious they adore their wives. All you have to do is watch the ways they look at them and your heart melts.

It's been such a blessing to have them in my life. I do not want to paint the picture of perfect lives for them. What is so beautiful is being able to witness their struggles and see them come out stronger as couples on the other side. A commonality I see in all of their marriages is how God is at the center of it all. It reinforces that God is the glue that holds it all together.

Marcus has been in my life for seven years and is the older brother I always wanted. I met his wife, Ashley, at a workout class she was teaching, and we became instant friends. She's so warm and inviting. She's created a welcoming, loving environment for their home, and when she asked me if I wanted to babysit their three kids, I didn't think twice. Their whole family is my family. My ex and I had recently broken up around the time Ashley and Marcus came into my life and Marcus was the example I needed at that moment. He constantly showed me what a faithful husband looked like. He adores Ashley and their kids. And he's not shy about leading them in faith and guides their kids in Bible truth. Witnessing their marriage at the time of my life when I felt broken gave me hope—hope for a future relationship that was similar to theirs. It was encouraging to see there are genuinely good guys in the world who want to selflessly love their family like Christ loves the church.

I hold these men close to me and need them to be present in my life regularly. When I'm feeling defeated, they remind me good men still exist. Good men who want to treat women well. Have a desire to provide for them and protect their hearts. I am blessed beyond measure to have these men around me, building me up, looking out for me as a daughter, granddaughter, and sister in Christ.

Sweet sisters, these types of men exist. These are the men

worth waiting for. These are the reasons why you desire to have standards and why settling would be so disappointing. It's my prayer that each one of you reading this book would be able to have at least one man like this to be a witness of God's love and goodness to you.

Reflection

Do you have good men in your life that you've been modeling your dating standard after? Yes_____ No_____

If yes, who are they? List them below.

What do you appreciate about those men in your life?

What do you appreciate about those men in your life?

Take Action

If you have good men in your life, pick up your phone right now and call or text them and tell them why they are awesome. Don't let another day go by without expressing your gratitude to them.

13

Still Single

"For we are God's masterpiece. He has created us anew in Christ Jesus, so we can do the good things he planned for us." Ephesians 2:10

Has anyone ever told you that you matter? You are so important, special, and unique. You are a gift made by God. He created you and you are made in his image. How amazing is that?

So what am I getting at? Your life has purpose. Yes, I said it. Your life has purpose. Having a relationship is not what defines you.

Some of you want me to say I have the happy love story ending with a hunky husband and some kids. You want to be able to read, "See girls, I found love and you can too!" But the truth is, I don't know your love story. I don't know what God has up his sleeve for you. But I know that what he has for you is good. So good. The truth is, I did find love, but not in the ways I expected to. Through my journey, I learned how to let my friends love me in a big way, and I've grown closer to my family members. Most importantly, I found total and complete love in Christ. His unconditional love is what gets me through the hard, lonely nights. I have all I need when I have him because I know everything I have in him, with him, and through him is perfect.

Maybe your husband is right around the corner. Maybe, little by little, you're growing more comfortable and happier with the idea of living a single life indefinitely. No matter where you are, I hope you've learned that you are worthy of living a life of happiness, passion, friendship, and love on many levels.

I love Jeremiah 29:10–14 from The Message Bible. It reads, "I'll show up and take care of you as I promised and bring you back home. I know what I'm doing. I have it all planned out—plans to take care of you, not abandon you, plans to give you the future you hope for. When you call on me, when you come and pray to me, I'll listen. When you come looking for me, you'll find me Yes, when you get serious about finding me and want it more than anything else, I'll make sure you won't be disappointed."

God just wants our hearts. He wants us to surrender to him, to come to him so he can bless us beyond all measure. Friend, I pray you can turn over the burden of your single life to him and allow him to carry that heavy load for you.

During this journey we've taken together, I hope you've learned a little more about yourself and the good things that are waiting for you. Make the jump. Do the big scary thing. Stop waiting and start living your purpose.

You are loved.
You are enough.
You are worthy.

Thank You!

Hey, sweet reader!

You're so awesome, and I can't put into words what it means to me to have you read my book. If you made it this far, I hope you loved it! If you think it could be valuable to other women, I'd love it if you'd head over to amazon.com and leave an honest review.

Thanks for your feedback! Please email me if you have any questions or want to know how to go deeper into igniting your worth!

www.igniteyourworth.com

igniteyourworth@gmail.com

Instagram: Clarissa_Christensen

Facebook: Clarissa_Christensen

Have you joined my free online community yet? Well what are you waiting for? **Facebook.com/groups/igniteyourworth**. Come together with other amazing women who want to encourage, support, and love you. You are welcome here, friend!

About the Author

Seven years ago, Clarissa Christensen took a big, scary leap and moved seven hours away from home to attend college. This changed the whole trajectory of her life for the better. While it opened up so many possibilities, she was initially bummed she did not earn her Mrs. degree.

Later she realized how fulfilling her life was and how worthy she is. Wanting others to come to that same realization, she became a licensed professional counselor and received her master's in counseling and development. To reach a wider audience and help more people, she wrote this book to prevent other women from suffering in their single life as long as she did.

She now embraces and enjoys her single life, and she wants all single women to realize they are worthy too and see all the adventure, passion, and purpose available to them right now.

To fulfill her passions, she enjoying playing around in make-up, changing her hair styles connecting with other empowered women. While trying to not keep up with the Kardashian's, she watches *Friends,* and drinks way too much coffee and chai tea lattes. And guess what? She enjoys all of that even while single.

facebook.com/clarissa.christensen.16

instagram.com/clarissa_christensen

Endnotes

6. To Be Seen

1. Guillaume Hanique, "Jessica Rey - The Evolution of the Swim Suit" (You-Tube, June 17, 2013), https://www.youtube.com/watch?v=WJVHRJbgLz8.

9. Finding Your Tribe

2. Original source unknown.

Made in the USA
Columbia, SC
21 February 2020